BEGINNING
TECHNICAL
MATHEMATICS
Made Easy

BEGINNING TECHNICAL MATHEMATICS

Made Easy

DAVID BRIANZA

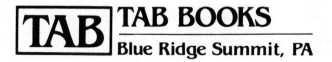

TAB BOOKS
Blue Ridge Summit, PA

FIRST EDITION
SECOND PRINTING

© 1990 by **TAB Books**.
TAB Books is a division of McGraw-Hill, Inc.

Printed in the United States of America. All rights reserved. The publisher takes
responsibility for the use of any of the materials or methods described in this bo
nor for the products thereof.

Library of Congress Cataloging-in-Publication Data

Brianza, David.
    Beginning technical mathematics made easy / by David Brianza.
        p.   cm.
    ISBN 0-8306-7383-0   —ISBN 0-8306-3383-9 (pbk.)
    1. Mathematics.   I. Title.
    QA39.2.B745   1989
    513′.12—dc20   89-36592
                                                             CIP

TAB Books offers software for sale. For information and a catalog, please conta
TAB Software Department, Blue Ridge Summit, PA 17294-0850.

Acquisitions Editor: Roland S. Phelps
Production: Katherine G. Brown

Contents

Introduction

The study of mathematics is of first-order importance in all areas of science and major human endeavors. The importance of the study of mathematics cannot be overstated. It is the very language of science. The word "science" derives from the Latin word "scire," meaning "to know." Knowledge is the product of science, and mathematics is the primary tool whereby that product is achieved.

The prospect of analysis becomes meaningless when divested of measurement. Simple yet profoundly meaningful questions, such as "how much," or "how often," etc., can only be answered by the numerical exactness of mathematical language. In order to be understood, the physical world must be quantified.

This very fact has served to foster an unfortunate, and for the most part, needless separation of those persons to whom math came relatively easy from those who were seemingly less fortunate. Indeed, you cannot help but wonder how many individuals, initially possessing great curiosity and interest in one or more areas of science or industry, have watched helplessly at those interests, together with the hopes they bore, dissolved amid the realization that the pursuit of their dream required proficiency in the subject they've always dreaded . . . mathematics. The individual, initially enthusiastic and eager, withdraws, uttering the lament of the academically vanquished: "Math has always been my worst subject."

It is my considered belief, based on experience, that such does not have to be the case at all. Many "seemingly less fortunate" persons are, in reality, not less fortunate at all, but simply weary of the pretentious, jargon-laden, unnecessarily technical manner in which most beginning math books are written. It is as if the book was written, not to instruct students, but to impress them.

Mathematics *can* be presented in a lucid, jargon-free, and non-intimidating style, one that is conducive unto learning. *Beginning Technical Mathematics Made Easy* provides a hand-in-hand tour, where the reader is shown in friendly and non-intimidating fashion how easy learning can be. The book offers a practical introduction to mathematics, and will impart to the reader proficiency in everything from basic arithmetic to advanced topics, such as algebra and graphing.

The purpose of the book is to impart the ability to understand technical, applied mathematics in the easiest, most unintimidating fashion possible. Replete with etymologies, concept histories, and many examples, *Beginning Technical Mathematics Made Easy* is unusually interesting for a mathematics book. There is nothing "assumed" on the part of the reader in regard to prior mathematical knowledge. Therefore, the most math-intimidated person, regardless of how lacking his or her technical background is, can expect to *understand* all areas of elementary mathematics and the manner in which they are employed. Because of the jargon-free, "friendly" manner in which it is written, students will find the book to be of great assistance regardless of whether it is used as the primary text in a formal course on mathematics, as a supplementary text in addition to the class text, or used alone, without benefit of an instructor.

The book anticipates the most commonly asked questions; a benefit derived from years of teaching experience on the part of the author. As a result, the student will be able to circumnavigate the common pit-falls by which so much time is needlessly lost. Also, you will acquire a greater sense of confidence when learning is easy. Spending inordinate amounts of time engaged in a struggling endeavor to understand material that you always believed you could never understand anyway only serves to fuel the fires of negative self-imagery. Such experience is hardly conducive to learning.

This book has been written to provide you with as enjoyable and painless a learning experience as possible. Its purpose then, apart from teaching mathematics, is to build confidence in the student by showing that technical mathematics is, in fact, not difficult. Individuals who believe they simply lack what it takes to become scientists or engineers might realize their goals after all.

1
Arithmetic

Virtually every area of advanced mathematics has its expedients, its shortcuts. Since much of what we call modern mathematics consists of concepts derived from previous concepts, which themselves existed as the outgrowth of still earlier concepts, it comes as no surprise that elementary mathematics is itself replete with expedients of its own.

FAST FIGURING

Multiplication is, in essence, "shortcut" addition. Note that 7×6 is the same as seven sixes, or $6 + 6 + 6 + 6 + 6 + 6 + 6$, which, when added a six at a time, gives 42. We, in order to avoid the necessity of counting and adding each digit, learn while still in grammar school the use and the idea behind multiplication tables.

Table 1-1

1	2	3	4	5	6	7	8	9	10
2	4	6	8	10	12	14	16	18	20
3	6	9	12	15	18	21	24	27	30
4	8	12	16	20	24	28	32	36	40
5	10	15	20	25	30	35	40	45	50
6	12	18	24	30	36	42	48	54	60
7	14	21	28	35	42	49	56	63	70
8	16	24	32	40	48	56	64	72	80
9	18	27	36	45	54	63	72	81	90
10	20	30	40	50	60	70	80	90	100

SHORTCUT MULTIPLICATION

When you want to know, for example, what 9 × 7 is equal to (referred to as the *product* of nine and seven), you simply locate the "9" in the left column, the "7" in the top column, then scan down from the top until you arrive at the number that is even with the "9"; that is 63.

In case you never thought of multiplication as being just a form of addition, you may obtain a "feel" for the addition aspect of multiplication by observing a few properties of the multiplication table. Notice the very top line, the numbers 1 to 10. Choose any one of these numbers, and then look at the column over which it sits. You will see that it is by *that* amount by which the column progresses; it is added to each number successively. Under the "5" column, the next number is 10, then 15, 5 is being added to each number, a continuing sum, all the way down the column, just as in the 7, 8, and 9 columns, the numbers under them grow in leaps of 7, 8, and 9. So it is with all columns.

Now look at the column running downward, on the left of the table. Again we find the numbers 1 through 10. And again, you'll find the process repeated . . . each number, proceeding from left to right, increases by the size of the number in the left column. So, you see that the multiplication table is, in reality, an addition table. If you multiply, say, 3 and 7, you may note under the "7" and in line with the "3" that "21" is found. But that 21 *became* 21 by starting as 3 in the left column, getting 3 added to it, becoming 6, etc., enabling us to see what "really" happened. The multiplication table simply did 3 + 3 + 3 + 3 + 3 + 3 + 3 for us.

There are a number of "tricks" you can call upon in order to help you multiply quickly and easily. For example, can you multiply 2,000 and 7,000 in your head? If you are like most people, you will say no. But you can. And it couldn't be easier. You know what 2 × 7 is. Of course, it's 14. Now, count the number of zeros in the entire problem. There are three in 2,000 and three more in 7,000, making a total of six zeros. That is how many will be in the answer, (the product) placed behind the 14: 14,000,000. Quickly and with no difficulty at all, we see that two thousand times seven thousand equals fourteen million.

What of 90 × 700? Start with 9 × 7, which is 63, to which you affix the zero found in "90" and the two in "700," getting 63,000. What could be easier?

The method you have been using, known as the "partial product" method, becomes only slightly more difficult when numbers that are not quite so "straightforward" are used. For example, take 73×8. You can make this problem easier by simply taking note of the fact that 73 is the same as $70 + 3$. Now, you are in a position to do the same thing you did with the easier numbers. Instead of 8×73, multiply $70 + 3$, $\times 8$, separately: $8 \times 7 = 56$, and there is one zero, giving 560. 8×3 is 24, and $560 + 24 = 584$, the correct answer.

For an additional example, do 25×7. First, 25 times 7 equals $20 + 5$, times 7. $7 \times 2 = 14$, and there is one zero. Hence, 140. Now, 7×5 equals 35, and $140 + 35 = 175$. Not a bad little method, wouldn't you say?

It was said at the beginning of the book that much of what we know today came to us by way of predecessor concepts, having themselves been derived from ideas predating them. In a sense, the later, newer concepts were "already there," waiting to be brought forth. This may be seen to be the case if you consider what happens when you read your multiplication table just *backwards* from the manner in which you normally read it. If you locate "9" on the left, and "3" atop, and then scan down the "3" column until you are even with the "9," you'll find "27," and at once realize that you have effectively multiplied 3 and 9. However, what if you *start* with the 27? Note that it lines up with the "9" on the left and the "3" on top. What is the significance of this?

There is considerable significance to this. For 27 divided by 9 is 3, and 27 divided by 3 is 9. So, you are led to the realization that, since looking at the table "backwards" results in division answers, then division must be multiplication in reverse. Just as addition is the opposite of subtraction (and vice-versa), so division is the opposite of multiplication. The four operations of addition, subtraction, multiplication and division are in reality *two* operations, each performed forward and backward. But remember . . . we said that multiplication was just fast addition. Well, if division is backwards multiplication, and multiplication is really addition, it follows that division is backwards addition, i.e., subtraction. How is this so?

Refer to Table 1-1 once again. In line with the "9" and under the "4" column, locate the number 36. The table shows that 36 divided by 9 equals 4. But how do we, in reality, *arrive* at that 4? The 4 comes about as the result of eight *subtractions* of 4 each, from 36. Or, to see it from another angle, use the table to show yourself that 36 divided by 4 equals 9. Now, from where does the 9 actually originate? Find 36 and count the number of columns on its left to the "9." There are three; 9 is the result of 3 subtractions of 9 each from 36.

The "melody" of the four operations is actually a variation on a single theme, by which you are provided an inkling of insight into the remarkable consistency of the number system.

Reducing the four arithmetical operations to one, namely subtraction, does not imply that subtraction dawned as the first discovered numerical operation. Early man, quite likely, happened upon some crude form of addition first, as simple progressive counting leads to higher and higher numbers, and as the number grows, addition is implied. Lacking a number system, as such, early man originated a type of counting system that persisted into relatively recent times, i.e., that of the Romans, in which stones were used to designate the quantity of a given set, such as, for example, the number of his animals. He simply gathered as many stones as he had animals, and, if at the end of the day comparison indicated a difference in the two groups, he knew he was missing animals. Incidentally, the use of stones for purposes of counting is the progenitor of our word "calculate," which derives from the Latin "calculus," and means, literally, "pebble," referring to the stones by which reckoning was accomplished.

Basic arithmetic, as you have seen, is logical and easy. And, what's more, the ease and logic carry right along into higher arithmatical processes.

EXERCISES

Use the *partial product* method to calculate the following:

1. 300 × 150
2. 3 × 3000
3. 25 × 50
4. 72 × 1000
5. 302 × 500
6. 130 × 100

2
Fractions

Practically everyone, at some point in their academic career was, or will be, necessitated to study fractions. It is easy to see why if you take but a moment to consider how important they really are. They're virtually everywhere. Your brand of gasoline sells for ninety one and nine-tenths cents per gallon. The loan on the house you have closed at twelve and three quarter percent interest. The recipe calls for a quarter cup of milk. Better get to a gas station, you're down to an eighth of a tank. On and on, you get the idea.

We're going to see just how easy it really is to work with fractions. In this section, you will proceed in step by step fashion, in which you will consider one area at a time. Start by considering the word "fraction" itself.

"Fraction" comes to us from the Latin "fractus," and means, literally, "broken." It is obvious as to why doctors refer to a broken bone as a "fracture," or why geologists may refer to "fractures" in the Earth's crust as the result of an Earthquake.

Numbers may also be fractured or broken. For example, the number "1" can be broken in half, so that it consists of two parts. Just as breaking a stick in half results in the creation of two halves of stick, so breaking the number 1 in half results in two halves, each equal in value to "$1/2$." Just as gluing the stick back together causes its two halves now to be one stick again, so adding $1/2$ and $1/2$ gives us our original number, 1, once more. How many "parts" can we break the number 1 into? How many pieces can you break the stick into?

ADDING FRACTIONS

How, exactly, does one go about adding those two one-halves? We've been told that one-half is written "1/2." The line under the "1" and above the "2" means division. So, when we write 1/2, we are saying, "one divided by two." Makes sense . . . if one orange is divided between two people, they each get one-half an orange. Now let's say that both of the people give back their orange halves . . . we add 1/2 and 1/2 and presumably, get one orange. Let's add, straight across, top and bottom numbers: One and one is two, and two and two is four; we now have 2/4. If we cut a circle into fourths, (imagine cutting a pizza into four large pieces) we may easily envision 2/4 as equaling 1/2. So, we know something is amiss here. How can one-half plus one-half equal one-half? Isn't that sort of thing like saying that three plus three equals three? What happened?

Nothing to be concerned about. We simply forgot one little step. Let's begin by setting the problem up. We wish to add the fractions one-half and one-half.

$$\frac{1}{2} + \frac{1}{2}$$

The fraction on the left, we'll just leave as is. It is the one on the right that we're interested in for the moment. We're going to take the bottom number, known as the denominator, and make a simple fraction out of it. The new fraction will have "2" both on top and as denominator:

$$\frac{2}{2}$$

Now, we're going to set it next to the fraction on the left, with a little "dot" between them:

$$\frac{1}{2} \cdot \frac{2}{2} + \frac{1}{2}$$

And now we'll do the same thing again, only reversed. Whereas last time we took the denominator from the right fraction, this time we'll take the denominator from the left fraction, make an entire fraction out of it, and place it on the right side:

$$\frac{1}{2} \cdot \frac{2}{2} + \frac{1}{2} \cdot \frac{2}{2}$$

The little dot means "multiply." Starting with the left side, $1 \times 2 = 2$, and for denominator, $2 \times 2 = 4$. So now we have

$$\frac{2}{4} + \frac{2}{2} \cdot \frac{1}{2}$$

which we multiply on the right side in the same way, giving

$$\frac{2}{4} + \frac{2}{4}$$

Now, all we have to do is add the top numbers, or numerators:

$$\frac{2 + 2}{4} = \frac{4}{4}$$

If you have four dollars and wish to divide it amongst four people, it's obvious that each person will get one dollar. So,

$$\frac{4}{4} = 1$$

For that matter, *any* number divided by itself will equal 1, whether it is 4 or 10,347,349, and for the same reason that the people referred to above each get a dollar.

Let's take another one. Let's add two fractions that do not have identical denominators, as the last two did. Let's try, say, $3/4$ and $1/5$.

First, we set the problem up:

$$\frac{3}{4} + \frac{1}{5}$$

Now we take the right fraction's denominator and make an entire fraction out of it, and set it near the left side:

$$\frac{3}{4} \cdot \frac{5}{5} + \frac{1}{5}$$

Next, we take the left fraction's denominator, make of it an entire fraction, and set it on the right side:

$$\frac{3}{4} \cdot \frac{5}{5} + \frac{1}{5} \cdot \frac{4}{4}$$

Now, we multiply: $3 \times 5 = 15$, and $4 \times 5 = 20$. So the left side becomes

$$\frac{15}{20} + \frac{1}{5} \cdot \frac{4}{4}$$

Multiplying the right side in the same fashion, numerator to numerator, denominator to denominator, we get

$$\frac{15}{20} + \frac{4}{20}$$

Since we're finished multiplying, we are now free to add. And since we now have denominators that are the same, we've managed to create what is known as the "common denominator," meaning we do not have to add them. Hence,

$$\frac{15}{20} + \frac{4}{20} \text{ is the same as } \frac{15 + 4}{20},$$

which, of course, equals

$$\frac{19}{20}$$

So, we may indicate that

$$\frac{3}{4} + \frac{1}{5} = \frac{19}{20}$$

So, now you see that it is not difficult at all to add fractions. All one needs to do is:

1. Make a fraction of the denominator of the right side fraction and put it on the left.
2. Make a fraction of the denominator of the left side fraction and put it on the right.
3. Multiply numerator to numerator, denominator to denominator.
4. Add the numerators.

Now perhaps you can see, regarding the first example, $1/2 + 1/2$, that it wasn't necessary to do the multiplication because we had a common denominator to start with:

$$\frac{1}{2} + \frac{1}{2} = \frac{1+1}{2} = \frac{2}{2} = 1$$

In any case involving different (unequal) denominators, we must do the multiplication as we've done in the foregoing. In this way, the common denominator is found.

SUBTRACTING FRACTIONS

What about subtraction of fractions? Nothing to worry about. No new procedures. It is the same thing as adding them, exactly, except that, as one might expect, we subtract instead of add.

For example, should we wish to subtract one-fourth from three-fourths, that is,

$$\frac{3}{4} - \frac{1}{4}$$

we would be enabled to see at a glance that the two fractions have common denominators. So, we may just subtract the numerators:

$$\frac{3-1}{4} = \frac{2}{4}$$

Both 2 and 4 are even numbers; they will divide evenly (no remainder) by 2.

Two divides by two once, four, twice. Hence, we may write $^2/_4$ as $^1/_2$. (Remember the pizza cut into four pieces.)

Now, what of the case involving subtraction of fractions not having identical denominators? Let's subtract

$$\frac{3}{4} - \frac{1}{2}$$

(1) Take the right side's denominator and make a fraction of it. Place it on the left side.

$$\frac{3}{4} \cdot \frac{2}{2} - \frac{1}{2}$$

(2) Take the left side fraction's denominator and make it a fraction. Place it on the right side.

$$\frac{3}{4} \cdot \frac{2}{2} - \frac{1}{2} \cdot \frac{4}{4}$$

(3) Multiply: Numerator to numerator, denominator to denominator, getting

$$\frac{6}{8} - \frac{4}{8}$$

(4) Subtract the numerators:

$$\frac{6 - 4}{8} = \frac{2}{8}$$

Two divides by two once, eight divides four times. Hence, $^2/_8$ is equal to $^1/_4$. As a result, we may write:

$$\frac{3}{4} - \frac{1}{2} = \frac{1}{4}$$

MULTIPLYING FRACTIONS

Multiplying fractions is easiest of all. No matter what the denominators, we simply multiply them straight across. This is one time in which we multiply both the numerator and denominator, without any "preliminaries." Suppose we wish to multiply

$$\frac{3}{4} \cdot \frac{3}{4}$$

(Remember, the little dot means "multiply.") Multiplying the numerators,

$$3 \times 3 = 9$$

multiplying the denominators,

$$4 \times 4 = 16$$

so,

$$\frac{3}{4} \cdot \frac{3}{4} = \frac{9}{16}$$

How about

$$\frac{3}{5} \cdot \frac{2}{7}$$

Same thing. We multiply, straight across, top and bottom:

$$\frac{3}{5} \cdot \frac{2}{7} = \frac{3 \cdot 2}{5 \cdot 7} = \frac{6}{35}$$

Reducing fractions is easy, too. If the numerator and denominator are even numbers, keep dividing by 2 until you can divide no further, then determine if another number is necessary to divide by. For example,

$$\frac{20}{30}$$

would reduce to

$$\frac{10}{15}$$

because two will divide twenty ten times, and thirty, fifteen times. Now, although two will divide ten evenly, it will not divide fifteen evenly.

Remember, we need a number that will divide *both* numerator and denominator, and leave no remainder. It has to divide them evenly. A moment's thought reveals that five will divide both ten and fifteen. Ten divided by five is 2, and fifteen divided by five is three. So, $^{10}/_{15}$ reduces to $^2/_3$. That's as far as you can take it.

DIVIDING FRACTIONS

So far, we have covered addition, subtraction, and multiplication of fractions, as well as reducing. Let us now consider division of fractions.

It is also quite easy. As formidable looking as something like:

$$\frac{\frac{2}{7}}{\frac{6}{11}}$$

may seem, there is really nothing to it. But we shall do something you may not expect. It may strike you as a bit odd, but in order to divide fractions, we *multiply* them.

We'll take the fraction on the bottom (in this case, the *whole fraction* is the denominator) and turn it over. That is, we will take $^6/_{11}$ and "turn it around" to $^{11}/_6$, then set it by the two-sevenths, and multiply, just as though it were a regular multiplication problem to begin with:

$$\frac{2}{7} \cdot \frac{11}{6}$$

Multiplying,

$$\frac{2 \cdot 11}{7 \cdot 6} = \frac{22}{42}$$

It's as easy as that. And since twenty-two divides by two, eleven times, and forty-two divides twenty-one times, we know that

$$\frac{22}{42} = \frac{11}{21}$$

We have easily concluded that

$$\frac{\dfrac{2}{7}}{\dfrac{6}{11}} = \frac{11}{21}$$

It was only necessary to take advantage of the fact that division is, in essence, just "backwards" multiplication. So, we turned our division problem backwards and multiplied.

Speaking of division, one item that many people seem to be at a loss to understand is why it is impossible to divide by zero. Whether it be in the numerator (such as $0/5$) or in the denominator, (i.e., $5/0$), the problem is rendered unsolvable. Why should this be?

Let's consider the zero first as the numerator. Why do mathematicians say that zero divided by any number is meaningless? It isn't hard to understand. Consider that if you have one dollar and wish to divide it five ways, each person will get $1/5$ dollar, or twenty cents. However, what if you had *no* money and wished to divide it five ways? Doesn't make much sense, does it? In fact, you could say that such a situation, since it cannot occur, is *meaningless*. So much for zero as the numerator.

It's a bit trickier when zero occupies the denominator. To most quickly and easily see what is happening, get your calculator. Let's take the fraction $1/6$. Press "1," "$\div$," then "6," now "$=$." The calculator will show 0.16666667 as result. Now press in $1/5$. You get 0.2, which is bigger than $1/6$, (by 1.2). If you enter $1/4$ into the calculator, you get 0.25, a value larger than $1/5$. Keep going . . . $1/3$, $1/2$ . . . each result is larger than the last. We see that the smaller the denominator becomes, the larger the result tends to be.

What happens, though, if the denominator starts to become *excessively* small? Punch $1/0.1$ into your calculator. The result is 10. 0.1 is equal to one-tenth, which is relatively small, but let's try another, still smaller number. Try $1/0.0001$. The result is 10,000.

INFINITY

Now, let's take one that is vanishingly small. Try $1/0.000000001$. Upon entering all those zeros into the calculator and pressing the "equals" button, the result is one *billion*. And so it continues . . . the closer the denominator gets to zero, the larger the result. It follows, then, that when the denominator *is* zero, the result is *infinitely* large.

It would take an entire book, and a large one at that, to so much as begin to adequately discuss how vast infinity is. No number that you could ever imagine, no matter how large, is anything but an immeasurably tiny fraction of infinity—an infinitely small fraction.

Consider a large number like one trillion, written as a one followed by no less than twelve zeros. It is a number so large that if you were to begin counting to it, starting from the number one, at the rate of a number per second, twenty-four hours a day, seven days a week, it would take you almost thirty-two years to reach it. Yet, it is no exaggeration to say that one trillion compares to infinity as a single atom compares to the entirety of the universe.

Obviously, such unfathomable vastness is of little information value in the course of daily affairs involving fractions, or virtually any other mathematical concept. *That* is why zero doesn't belong in the denominator.

Now that you know how to add, subtract, multiply and divide fractions, all you need is practice, through which you will gain confidence and speed. In order to facilitate your acquisition of these two worthwhile attributes, the following exercises are presented. Refer to the material in this section for help whenever you feel the need. Answers to exercises appear at the back of the book.

EXERCISES

1. Add one-third and one-third.

2. $2/7 + 2/7$

3. $3/4 + 3/5$

4. $5/9 + 9/5$

5. $11/16 + 3/11$

---

1. Subtract one-fourth from three-fourths.

2. $5/7 - 2/7$

3. $7/9 - 5/11$

4. $6/13 - 2/5$

5. $7/71 - 3/34$

---

1. Multiply two-fifths and seven-eighths.

2. $5/9 \cdot 6/7$

3. $30/31 \cdot 51/52$

4. $75/94 \cdot 2/3$

5. $24/29 \cdot 6/41$

---

1. Divide five-sixths by three-fourths.

2.

$$\frac{\frac{2}{3}}{\frac{3}{4}}$$

3.

$$\frac{\frac{57}{2}}{\frac{1}{11}}$$

Reduce the following fractions:

1. $3/9$

2. $15/20$

3. $100/200$

4. $7/21$

5. $2/4$

3
Percentages

The word "percent" means "by the hundred." The second syllable of the word "cent" originates from the Latin "centum," and, meaning "one hundred," is the origin of such words as "century," "centennial," "centipede," etc., all of which convey meanings centered around the quantity one hundred.

Resultantly, when we refer, for example, to twenty-five percent of an overall whole, we are saying "twenty-five hundredths," or "twenty-five out of every one hundred."

The symbol "%" is, itself, a sort of slurred "100." The "1" has evolved into a line, or bar, separating the two zeros.

Other such symbols have similarly "slurred" their way into being, having originated with the early Romans. For example, when a Roman author wished to convey exclamation, the appropriate sentence was followed with "io." This, however, was unclear to the reader, who had a tendency to confuse the word with the rest of the text, and miss its intended meaning. To end the confusion, "io" was spelled vertically, with the "i" above the "o," an arrangement whose eventual evolution ultimately resulted in the advent of our "!" (exclamation point).

In dealing with percentages, one is dealing with segments, portions of a whole. In the example used above, it was stated that twenty-five percent of a quantity is the same as saying "25 out of every one hundred." Because twenty-five one-hundredths ($^{25}/_{100}$) reduces to $^1/_4$, we are led to the realization that "twenty-five out of every one hundred" is exactly equal to "one out of every four," which may be represented graphically as:

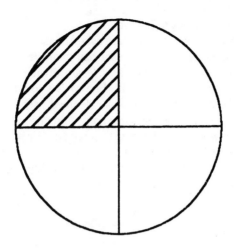

Fig. 3-1

This is, in essence, a "picture" of what twenty-five percent looks like, from which it is easy to reason what fifty, seventy-five, and one hundred percent would look like as well.

The operations involved in order to determine percentages are basic and simple. For example, let us imagine a situation in which all the information we have is that a certain technician performed analysis on 20% of the sample stock, consisting of, originally, 35 samples. How many samples did the technician analyze?

First, 20% = $^{20}/_{100}$.
Multiplying,

$$\frac{20}{100} \cdot \frac{35}{1} = \frac{700}{100} = 7$$

telling us the number of samples analyzed. In dealing with percents, multiplication is the order of the day.

Simple multiplication percentage problems may disguise themselves somewhat, but once you have learned the basics of what is transpiring, you will easily see through the problem. Consider, for example, a situation in which you, as a salesperson, have sold $3,000 worth of merchandise. Assuming that you are entitled to 3% of your overall sales volume, how much money do you have coming?

This is the same problem as worked in the example above; only the numbers and situation are different.

$$3\% \frac{3}{100} = .03 \qquad .03 \cdot 3,000 = \$90.00$$

what you should expect to receive.

Now, let us imagine that you are asked to assist in figuring percentages. Your laboratory supervisor has requested that you note how many beakers of a particular size are etched, or otherwise damaged, out of an overall amount. She wishes to know what percentage of the beakers are no longer deemed useable, for a cost survey in regard to budgeting. How do you proceed?

First, you will need to know the overall number of beakers. Let us say that there are 300. Of that amount, determine how many are considered no longer useable, e.g., 25. Dividing the smaller amount by the larger,

$$\frac{25}{300} = \frac{1}{12} = 0.08333.$$

Because percentage deals with numbers "by the hundreds," we will multiply the decimal value by that amount:

$$100 \cdot 0.08333 = 8.333$$

showing that of the 300 beakers, 8 $1/3$ percent of them are no longer in service.

To determine what percentage a smaller number is of some larger number, divide the smaller by the larger, and multiply by 100:

$$\frac{\text{smaller}}{\text{larger}} \times 100 = \frac{\text{percentage that the}}{\text{smaller is of the larger}}$$

For example, what percent of 27 is 3?

$$\frac{3}{27} \times 100 = 11^{1}/_{9}$$

In some instances, multiplication and division are both needed to solve particular problems. Consider that a certain salesman earned $90 commission, as the result of being entitled to keep 2% of what he sells. How much did he sell?

We know that 2% of some unknown number equals $90. If we let "x" represent, for the moment, that unknown amount, we may set the problem up in such a way as that the question virtually answers itself.

First, we know that 2% means two-hundredths, or $^2/_{100}$, which equals 0.02. So, we may state

$$0.02 \cdot x = \$90$$

The value of x may be determined by dividing

$$x = \frac{\$90}{0.02} = \$4,500,$$

showing just how easy it really is to determine percentages. Consider some additional examples:

Example: A person received an 11.5% raise. As a result, she will receive an extra $140.00. How much was her original salary?

$$11.5 \cdot x = 140$$

$$x = \frac{140}{1} \cdot \frac{100}{11.5} = \frac{14,000}{11.5} = \$1217.39$$

Example: If the tip given to the server in a restaurant equals three dollars and represents 15% of the price of the meal, how much did the meal cost?

$$15\% \cdot x = \$3.00$$

$$x = \frac{\$3.00}{0.15} = \$20.00$$

Example: Your check at a restaurant totals $4.42. The city in which the restaurant is located charges 7% tax. What was the price of the meal?

$$
\begin{aligned}
\text{meal} + \text{tax} &= \$4.42 \\
x + 0.07x &= \$4.42 \\
1.07x &= \$4.42 \\
x &= \frac{\$4.42}{1.07} = \$4.13 \\
\text{Tax} &= \$0.29 \\
\\
\text{Meal} &= \$4.13
\end{aligned}
$$

THE PIE GRAPH

Percentages, represented graphically, are helpful in allowing one to form a picture, and aid to understanding. For example, a household with a total income of $3,500 per month may arrange its budget such that 10% of earnings are devoted toward grocery expenditures, 25% toward mortgage payments, 15% toward transportation costs, 30% toward debts, another 10% for clothing, with the final 10% going for general household expenses. Such a situation may be represented:

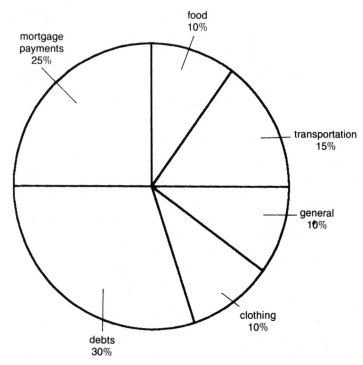

Fig. 3-2

Such a graph is known as a "pie chart," due to the obvious resemblance. It is useful in all areas of business, budgeting, personnel allocations, etc., and is but one example of the usefulness provided by the ability to calculate percentages. For example, the above chart instantly makes quite clear the fact that the family to whom it refers is heavily in debt, and perhaps ought to reconsider some of their spending habits.

EXERCISES

1. Represent the number "3" as a percentage.

2. You have sold $50.00 worth of goods at 5% commission. How much have you earned?

3. What percentage of 75 is 5?

4. You have analyzed 15% of the existing sample stock, meaning that you have analyzed 30 samples. How many samples were there originally?

5. You are promised a 7% raise. Assuming that your salary is $200.00 per week now, how much extra can you look forward to?

6. The tip is $2.50, and is 12% of the bill. What is the overall bill?

7. On a pie chart, represent the following:
   A company has divided its labor force such that:

   (a) 25% are production personnel.
   (b) 15% are kitchen help.
   (c) 20% are maintenance workers.
   (d) 5% are supervisors.
   (e) 2% are custodians.
   (f) 3% are watchmen/security.
   (g) 10% are secretarial.
   (h) 15% are salespersons.
   (i) 5% are executives.

8. If the above company employs 280 people, how many of them are production personnel? Executives?

4
Exponents

The word "exponent" is a composite of two Latin words, and comes to us as their derivative. The first part of the word, "ex," means "out," while the second part, "pon," means "place." In combining them, we are told of something that is "placed out," which is exactly what an exponent is, in relation to its main number, or base. For example, in the expression 10^3, read as "ten to the third power" or "ten cubed," the small 3, written as a superscript, is the exponent, the number "placed out" from 10, its base, and tells us how many times the base is to be raised, or multiplied, by itself. "Ten to the third power" is equivalent to $10 \times 10 \times 10$; three successive multiplications of ten, which gives 1,000. Hence, we may indicate that $10^3 = 1,000$, just as ten to the second power, or ten squared, 10^2, is the same as 10×10, and equals 100.

Notice that when dealing with the base 10, there is a certain consistency. The exponent is equal to the number of zeros there are in the number, fully written out. Recall that $10^3 = 1,000$, $10^2 = 100$. This holds for *any* power to which ten is raised. For example, 10^5 is written as a one followed by five zeros; one hundred thousand. 10^6 denotes a quantity written as a one followed by six zeros, or one million. Ten raised to *whatever* power is equal to and can be written as a one followed by *whatever* number of zeros.

When working with extremely large numbers, you quickly begin to see the value of such a system, a sort of mathematical shorthand, known as "exponential notation." Imagine how cumbersome and time consuming it would be were you constrained to write out, in numbers, such a figure as ten quadrillion. Contrast such inconvenience with the ability to quickly write ten quadrillion as 10^{16}. When you stop to consider that 10^{16} is, in science, a rather small number, (consider, for example, that there are 2.500,000,000,000,000,000 atoms in a single gram of plutonium. This huge number is read as two thousand five hundred billion billion, and is 250,000 times larger than ten quadrillion) you begin to appreciate all the more such shorthand. Whether it be a discussion of astronomical distances or the number or size of molecules or atoms, exponential notation is indispensible.

Exponential notation allows for the easy and rapid handling of extremely large or excessively small numbers. Where the bases are the same, one need but perform very simple maneuvers on the exponents. For example, let us multiply $10^3 \times 10^3$, or $1,000 \times 1,000$. For a moment, recall the first section of the book, wherein you learned the "partial product" method of multiplication, in which you multiplied the non-zero numbers, and then added all the zeros. In the case of $1,000 \times 1,000$, $1 \times 1 = 1$, and there are six zeros, giving $1,000,000$, showing that the method works for exponents. Now, notice the two exponents in the two expressions, 10^3 and 10^3. Each one, as already pointed out, is the number of zeros contained in the fully written out number. Beginning to get the idea? If you're thinking that all one need do is to add the exponents, i.e., $10^3 \times 10^3$ $= 10^{3+3} = 10^6$, you're right. The only stipulation involved with such a maneuver is that the bases be equal. For example $10^4 \times 3^3 \neq$ (does not equal) 10^{4+3}, or 10^7. However, $3^3 \times 3^7$ *does* equal 3^{10}.

Since all of mathematics is a system of shorthand, involving particular symbols, let us write this property of exponents and bases in equation style. Letting "b" stand for "base" and x,y for exponents, we may indicate

$$b^x \cdot b^y = b^{x+y}$$

and designate this as our first rule of exponents. The little dot "$\cdot$" is an algebraic symbol, and means multiply.

We started out using multiplication as a means by which to effect speedy addition. When it comes to exponents, we find ourselves using addition to increase the speed of multiplication. But, remember . . . we were able to show multiplication to be "backwards" division, and division to be a form of subtraction. Bearing this in mind, let's see what happens to our exponents when we divide. Let's try

$$\frac{10^6}{10^3}$$

23

which means exactly the same thing as

$$1,000 \sqrt{1,000,000}$$

and results in

$$
\begin{array}{r}
1,000 \\
1,000\overline{\smash{\big)}1,000,000} \\
\underline{1,000,00} \\
0
\end{array}
$$

which we know is equal to 10^3. It looks as though 3 was subtracted from the exponent "6" of the numerator. And that is exactly the case, because

$$\frac{10^6}{10^3} = 10^{6-3} = 10^3$$

showing that our thinking of division as a form of subtraction is perfectly valid, especially where exponents are concerned. So, we may write our second rule of exponents:

$$\frac{b^x}{b^y} = b^{x-y}$$

NEGATIVE EXPONENTS

The second rule states that the exponent in the denominator is to be subtracted from the exponent in the numerator. This implies that the numerator exponent (x) is larger than that of the denominator, (y). What of the case in which this is not true? Instead of $10^6/10^3$, what if we have

$$\frac{10^3}{10^6}$$

Not to worry; one may proceed as usual. Our rule holds up. We simply make one small alteration.

Since

$$
\begin{array}{r}
0.001 \\
1,000,000 \overline{\smash{\big)}1,000} \\
\underline{1,000} \\
0
\end{array}
$$

which is the same as our original answer, 1,000, with the exception that 1 has been divided by it, (that is, $0.001 = 1/1,000$), we simply incorporate the one into our result.

Consequently, as

$$\frac{10^3}{10^6} = \frac{1}{1,000} \, ,$$

we know that, in general,

$$\frac{10^x}{10^y} = \frac{1}{10^{y-x}} \text{ where } y^* > x$$

For example,

$$\frac{10^5}{10^7} = \frac{1}{10^{7-5}} = \frac{1}{10^2}$$

which is equivalent to 0.01.

When "1" is situated as numerator over *any* number, the number over which it sits is said to be "reciprocated." Hence, when the exponent y is greater than the exponent x, we simply proceed as we did where x is greater than y, and reciprocate the result.

We have seen thus far what happens regarding multiplication and addition of exponents. Now, let us consider the case of an exponent raised to the power of *another* exponent.

THE POWER OF A POWER

We've seen what happens when 10 is raised to the sixth power, as 10^6. But we haven't as yet seen what to do in the event the power *itself* is raised to a power, i.e.,

$$10^{6^2}$$

Such operation is as easy as the others. In order to arrive at the answer, we simply multiply the exponents. $6 \times 2 = 12$, so

$$10^{6^2} = 10^{12}$$

---

*The symbol ">" is read "greater than." Conversely, "<" is read "less than."

Since raising *any* number to the second power involves multiplying that number by itself, a process described as "squaring," then one may easily see that what we did was to quickly and easily find the square of one million. Should we wish to know the square of any large number, all we need do is think of that number in exponential form, and multiply its exponent by 2. For example, we are now able to see at a glance that 1,000 squared is $10^{3 \cdot 2} = 10^6$, or one million. Since 10^3 squared is one million, it follows that one thousand (10^3) is the *square root* of one million. And so it goes. To raise a number to the third power is to "cube" that number. Hence,

$$10^{3^3}, \text{ (read as ten to the third to the third)}, = 10^{3 \cdot 3}$$

which is 10^9, showing that one thousand cubed equals one billion, suggesting, of course, that one thousand is the *cube root* of one billion.

Knowing now that a power raised to the power of another power (or, an exponent raised to the power of another exponent) is brought about by multiplying the two exponents, we may formalize yet another rule regarding exponents:

$$b^{x^y} = b^{x \cdot y}$$

5
Negative Numbers

The concept of negative numbers may be one by which you, as is the case with many others, are troubled. "How there can be a number less than *nothing* I do not understand," you may say. "It seems in violation of common sense."

A moment's thought will reveal that it isn't. The concept of negative numbers is one that is most useful, and quite common. Indeed, though you may not be aware of it, you deal with negative numbers, or at least their equivalent, virtually every day of your life.

The most obvious example of the usefulness of numbers less than zero is found on a common thermometer. We readily comprehend what is meant when we are told of a temperature that is less than zero. Zero is seen as simply that by which the temperatures above zero are separated from those below it.

The manner in which the average person tends to define "zero" makes for an error, the result of which does much to foster difficulty in thinking about negative numbers. Most people regard zero as representing "nothing," a sort of abstract, fathomless void. "Hence," they reason, "there cannot be numbers less than zero because that implies the existence of something that is less than nothing." Although such argument, at first glance, sounds reasonable, in fact it is not. It is built entirely upon a false premise.

Zero is, in fact, a *number*. That this is so may be realized if you will just engage in a brief thought experiment. Imagine that you have an account at a particular bank. In this account, you, at present, have no money. Even so, you do, nevertheless, have an account, one which has a balance of zero dollars. Contrast this with another bank at which you have no account. There, you indeed have nothing.

Zero is a figure, a number, one that like any other, represents the amount of money in your account. If your balance were nothing, you would not *have* an account.

When you are told by the weatherman that it is zero degrees outside, you do not take this to mean that there is no temperature.

So . . . zero is not "nothing." It simply represents a quantity that is definable as "empty." Indeed, the zero, as a number, originated with the ninth century Hindus, who designated the symbol by which it was represented as "sunya," meaning "empty." Distortion via the Arabic "zefirum," also meaning "empty," resulted ultimately in the advent of our word "zero," symbolized as "0," by which emptiness is depicted. Note that "emptiness," is not synonymous with "nothingness."

Zero holds a place of distinction. On the number line, zero marks the dividing point, either side of which separate infinities begin: the infinity of the positive numbers and the infinity of the negative numbers.

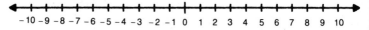

Fig. 5-1

The arrows at either end of the line indicate that the line expands unboundedly (infinitely) in either direction. As we proceed from left to right, anywhere on the line, the numbers increase in size. Proceeding from right to left, the numbers are seen to decrease. This implies, for example, that -6 is less than -5, which is less than -3, etc. So, in the case of the negatives, the larger the number the smaller it is, as it is headed in the opposite direction from zero, the farther from which it gets, the smaller it becomes.

As a footnote, it was told to you that the symbol " $>$ " is to be read "greater than." One needn't look too closely in order to discern that the symbol is actually an arrow. The arrow is pointing to the right, the significance of which is to designate that the number to which it refers is found, on the number line, to the right of another number. Any number that is situated to the right of another number is greater than ($>$) that number, as is easily seen on the number line. A similar argument holds for the " $<$ " symbol.

Ever since negative numbers were put into systematic use by the Italian mathematician Girolamo Cardano, about 1550, they have been most useful, indeed, even enlightening. When physicist Paul

Dirac, in 1930, received a negative number as the outcome to a particular equation he had set up regarding the phenomena of the subatomic world, anti-matter was predicted, and subsequently, just two years later, found. Negative numbers tell of rates of descent, decreasing velocity and much more. Indeed, they even provide us with means whereby to answer our skeptic who so assuredly informs us that it is impossible to have less than no money at all. Indeed, it most certainly *is* possible. Imagine yourself in debt to the amount of five dollars. To be in debt five dollars is, in essence, to have five dollars less than no dollars at all. Viewed in this context, the thought of there existing a quantity less than zero becomes endowed with a tangible, graspable reality.

Some of the operations regarding negative numbers might, at first, seem confusing. For example, one may question the rule which states that a positive number minus a negative number always results in a positive number, saying that there does not appear to be any obvious reason as to why this should be so. For example,

$$5 - -6 = 11$$

Why should this be so?

In order to get a feel for the logic involved here, let us view this conceptually, and again consider you as having a five dollar debt. Now, imagine that a friend pays the debt *for* you. In other words, your friend has subtracted from you one debt on the order of five dollars. Having had the debt subtracted from you, you are, of course, minus the debt, which in reality means that you are five dollars ahead. By subtracting the negative (owed) five dollars, you emerge as being five dollars ahead, just as if your friend had directly given you the money. Perhaps now you are better enabled to visualize how a number, minus a negative number has a positive number for result.

In the same manner, one can easily be made to see how adding a negative number to any number is the same as *subtracting* by the amount of the negative number.

That is, for example,

$$10 + -6 = 10 - 6 = 4$$

If you had the sum of ten dollars, and someone, somehow managed to give you (to *add* to you) a six dollar debt, you would be reduced to four dollars.

Multiplication of two negative numbers always results in a positive number. However, unlike the previous examples, the reason for this is difficult to visualize; real world examples are without meaning in this situation. For example, it is meaningless to speak of four negative dollars, or negative four dollars, being owed by negative 2 men.

The reason for the rule whereby the multiplication of two negatives results in a positive is purely mathematical. Adopted by mathematicians of antiquity in an attempt to establish consistency, the seemingly arbitrary rule did away with certain contradictions in the system.

A negative number, multiplied by a positive number, is always negative. Just as, for example, 3×5 equals three fives, so 3×-5 equals three *negative* fives, or -15. For this reason, an *uneven* number of multiplications of a negative number by itself will also result in a negative, in seeming contradiction to what was explained regarding the multiplication of two negatives, above. However, there is, in reality, no contradiction at all. The mathematicians referred to above said that two negatives when multiplied result in a positive. From this it has been extrapolated that any *even* number of multiplications will result in a positive number. Not too surprising, when seen in light of the realization that all even numbers are multiples of two. All uneven numbers of multiplication will produce a negative. For example, we know that $-2 \times -2 = 4$. But $-2 \times -2 \times -2 = -8$, since this is the same as first multiplying -2×-2, which gives us (positive) four, and then multiplying that positive four by -2, resulting in the multiplication of a positive and a negative, and producing -8 for the answer.

As we did with the exponents, we may set what we've determined thus far in the language of symbols. We'll let the letter "n" stand for "number," and indicate:

$$-n \cdot -n = +n$$

which is to say, a negative number times a negative number equals a positive number.

Similarly,

$$-n \cdot +n = -n$$

and

$$n - -n = +n$$

The rules apply for the division of signed numbers:

$$\frac{-n}{-n} = +n \qquad \frac{-n}{n} = -n \qquad \frac{n}{-n} = -n$$

It is not necessary to place a "plus" sign (+) in front of a number to show that the number is positive. Just the absence of the negative sign (−) implies that the number is positive.

As a result of having become versed in negative numbers, we may now somewhat simplify the rule regarding the division of exponents on page that indicates

$$\frac{10^x}{10^y} = \frac{1}{10^{y-x}} \text{ where } y > x$$

Now, when faced with the need to subtract a larger exponent from a smaller one, we need not resort to reciprocals. We may now employ negative numbers as exponents. For example,

$$\frac{10^3}{10^6} = 10^{3-6} = 10^{-3}$$

which provides us with our cue to begin discussion on the significance of negative exponents.

What, exactly, is the difference between a positive and a negative exponent? The difference, though important, is simple. Remember that we defined reciprocation as being the result of dividing 1 into any number? For example, if we start with the number 4, and divide 1 into it, i.e., $1/4$, we have *reciprocated* the 4. And so it is with any number. If we start with 2,377.26 and divide it into 1, as $1/2,377.26$, we have the *reciprocal* of 2,377.26. Well, a negative exponent is simply the reciprocal of the same number in positive form. For example, you will recall that when we divided

$$\frac{10^6}{10^3}$$

we got

$$\frac{10^3}{10^6} = 10^{6-3} \cdot 10^3 = 1,000$$

However, when we divided

$$\frac{10^3}{10^6} \text{ , we got } \frac{10^3}{10^6} = \frac{1}{10^{6-3}} = \frac{1}{1,000} = 0.001 \text{ ,}$$

because we reciprocated by dividing with 1, as a result of the rule. Now, because we are able to use negative exponents, we may proceed

$$\frac{10^3}{10^6} = 10^{3-6} = 10^{-3} = 0.001$$

So, you see, the negative exponent did the job of dividing by the 1, or reciprocating, for us. Hence, we may say that 10^{-3} is the reciprocal of 10^3, or, in English, one thousandth is the reciprocal of one thousand.

In mathematical notation, the exponent $^{-1}$ reciprocates *any* number or fraction. Therefore, just as we may correctly indicate 10^{-3} as equaling 0.001, or the reciprocal of 1,000 (10^3) so we may write

$$1,000^{-1} \text{ or } 10^{3^{-1}}$$

and obtain the same result. Why? Because 1,000 is exactly the same as 10^3, as we've long since established. Reciprocating 10^3, as we did above, $(10^3)^{-1}$, we need but recall the rule pertaining to the raising of an exponent to the power of an exponent. Recall that in order to do so, we multiplied the two exponents. In this case, that gives us

$$10^{3^{-1}} = 10^{-3}$$

which is what we started with. *That* is how the exponent works. Because of the law of signs whereby the multiplication of a positive number and a negative number result in a negative number, 10^3 becomes 10^{-3}.

Incidentally, reciprocation is the process by which fractions are inverted. If we take a fraction, for example $2/3$, and turn it around to $3/2$, we have reciprocated that fraction. So, in the section on fractions in which we found that division of fractions is accomplished by inverting and multiplying, we were actually reciprocating the fraction in the denominator position. In symbols, we may describe such action as

$$\left(\frac{a}{b}\right)^{-1} = \frac{b}{a}$$

For example,

$$\left(\frac{3}{4}\right)^{-1} = \frac{4}{3}$$

EXERCISES

Reciprocate the following:

1. 3

2. 64

3. $3/7$

4. a/b

5. $1/27$

6. $a/3b$

6
Scientific Notation

When René Descartes, in 1637, first suggested that the power to which a number was raised could be written as a superscripted number beside it, it is doubtful that even he could have envisioned just how useful his idea of exponents would later become or how much it would evolve into. Since numbers can be as simple or as complex, literally, as we care to make them, it is obvious that a system is required whereby simplicity or complexity can be handled with equal ease. Such, indeed, is the case with that form of shorthand, a variation on exponential notation, known as scientific notation.

Obviously, when routinely working with numbers, you expect to be called upon to employ numbers other than the nice, round ones we've been using so far, like 1,000 or 100. How, for example, do you go about expressing out of the ordinary though descriptive numbers as, say, that figure by which is given the volume of the sun? Or, how about the volume of a proton, one of the constituents of the atomic nucleus? No doubt, one is going to be excessively large, the other vanishingly small. If we retain our system of raising the base of ten to some power, apparently we are going to have to multiply it by some value in order to obtain an expression that accurately conveys our intended meaning.

Let us see what happens should we begin so multiplying. Since we've been working with 10^3, or one thousand, for a while, let's do so a bit longer, and experiment.

Obviously, any number multiplied by 1 results in the same number with which you started; multiplication by 1 does not alter anything. Since, for example, $1 \times 5 = 5$, multiplication of an exponentially written number, such as 10^3, by 1 does not change it:

$$1 \times 10^3 = 1,000$$

Should you desire to express "2,000" exponentially, you might guess that "two one-thousands" would convey your meaning. And you'd be right:

$$2 \times 10^3 = 2,000$$

The same for three thousand, four thousand, etc., whatever multiple of 1,000 required, all you need do is multiply by the number of the desired multiple.

Once again, though, we are forced to contend with the fact that not all numbers that we are necessitated to write can be written as clean multiples of some convenient number like 1,000. How, for example, do you go about expressing such a number as 2,250,000?

Once again, of course, we will need to multiply. Since there are six decimal places to the right of the first number, we know that we are dealing with a multiple of one million. (The number itself tells us that; 2,250,000 is pronounced as "two *million*, two hundred and fifty thousand"). So, we may begin by writing

$$\times 10^6$$

as we know that the number we seek is, as stated, a multiple of one million. Since we know, in part, what that multiple is, specifically 2, we may indicate

$$2 \times 10^6$$

which we know indicates two million. We are, at this point, getting close. We need to get the 250,000 into the expression.

We might reason that 250,000 is one-quarter of a million. One quarter of *anything* is, of course, one-fourth, written $1/4$, and has for decimal equivalent the value 0.25. Putting that into our expression, we arrive at

$$2.25 \times 10^6$$

the correct answer.

Another way in which we might proceed is to simply ask ourselves what number is it, when multiplied by one million (10^6) equals two million, two hundred fifty thousand?

We'll set our question in the form of an equation, and let "n" represent the number we seek. Recalling that the little dot "·" means multiply, we write

$$10^6 \cdot n = 2{,}250{,}000$$

which simply says, "one million, multiplied by a certain number, n, equals two million, two hundred and fifty thousand."

Recall that we discovered that multiplication is backward division. Since we wish to know what to multiply by, we'll "undo" the multiplication in our question/equation via division. We'll set the number on the right of the equals sign as the numerator, the 10^6 as denominator:

$$n = \frac{2{,}250{,}000}{10^6} = 2.25$$

Notice something here that will serve to greatly simplify and speed up your ability to divide. The denominator, 10^6, indicates, as you know, a number with *six* decimal places: 1,000,000. Upon dividing by it, above, we see that our answer is the same number that we started out with for the numerator, 2,250,000, with the exception that the decimal point has been moved to the left *six* places. Since, behind the decimal point, all the zeros in the world wouldn't make one bit of difference, we just drop them.

If the decimal point moves to the left upon dividing, then, since division is backwards multiplication, it follows that multiplication will cause the decimal point to move to the right. For example, in 100 × 2.50, we see that there are two decimal places in the 100. All we need to do is simply shift our decimal point to the right two places, to arrive at the correct answer: 250.

Returning to the problem at hand, we now know what number it is, which when multiplied by 10^6, equals 2,250,000. It is 2.25:

$$2.25 \times 10^6 = 2{,}250{,}000$$

Now for a little terminology. The whole number on the left of the decimal point in an expression such as the one above, is known as the "characteristic." It is the portion of the expression whereby its particular "individuality," its "character" is determined. The decimal portion, to the right of the decimal point, is called the "mantissa," a word which comes directly from Latin, and means "an addition," a "makeweight," signifying its relationship unto the characteristic. In the expression 2.25×10^6, "2" is the characteristic, with ".25" the mantissa, "adding weight" to the characteristic, helping it to achieve the value that is required, the full 2,250,000.

In dealing with exponents of the base ten, meaning that every expression we write using it will be some multiple of ten, we are given some flexibility regarding where we place the decimal point. Hence, we may easily perform operations whereby the numbers (characteristic and mantissa) are changed, and still have the same answer with which we started (2,250,000). All that is required when we move the decimal point is that we remember to change the exponent. For example, if we move the decimal point one place to the left, and make our current characteristic and mantissa, 2.25, into .225, we simply increase the exponent by 1, so that we have

$$0.225 \times 10^7$$

If we were to move it one place yet farther to the left (which, in order to do so necessitates that we insert a zero as a "place holder") we simply raise the exponent by yet one more:

$$.0225 \times 10^8$$

Do you see the emergence of a pattern here? For every place that the decimal point is moved to the *left* the exponent goes *up* by one:

$$0.0025 \times 10^9$$

This is because the number that we are multiplying by becomes smaller and smaller as the decimal point moves to the left. As a result, the number by which it is multiplied (ten raised to increasing powers) must increase in order to compensate. Above, two hundred, twenty five thousandths (0.225) is multiplied by ten million in order to get, for the product, 2,250,000.

As you might expect, moving the decimal point to the *right* results in the *lowering* of the exponent. For each decimal place to the right that the decimal point is moved, the exponent is reduced by 1. Hence,

$$0.00225 \times 10^9 \text{ becomes } 0.225 \times 10^7,$$

just as

$$2.25 \times 10^6 = 22.5 \times 10^5 = 225 \times 10^4 = 2,250 \times 10^3 =$$

$$22,500 \times 10^2, \text{ etc.}$$

Any number raised to the first power, is not changed. It remains exactly what it started out as. Hence, $10^1 = 10$, just as $3^1 = 3$, or $427^1 = 427$. So,

$$225,000 \times 10^1$$

is the same as

$$225,000 \times 10, \text{ which equals } 2,250,000.$$

Any number raised to the power of zero equals 1, no matter what number it is. Whether it be ten, or six hundred quintillion, if it is raised to the zero power, it is equal to 1:

$$10^0 = 1, 600,000,000,000,000,000,000^0 = 1$$

So, $2,250,000 \times 10^0 = 2,250,000 \times 1 = 2,250,000$, the number we started out with, demonstrating that with scientific notation, a lot of flexibility is indeed possible. Further, it provides us with the key whereby to easily determine how to write any number in scientific notation, a statement that will be made clear a little later. For now, just remember that for every place the decimal is moved to the left, the exponent goes up one in value, and vice-versa. In order to facilitate your remembering this rule, think of the phrase, "if it is *left up* to me, I'll be *right down*."

We shall now consider what to do in order to convert a large number into scientific notation. Let us take the number 337,700,000,000,000,000. First, we shall exclude the number on the left, the first "3," and count the number of digits following it.

We see that there are, not counting the three, 17 digits. So, we will write

$$\times\ 10^{17}$$

Now, we shall take the "3" we've been ignoring, place a decimal point after it, and then use the first three numbers following the "3." Upon combining with our base and exponent, we have

$$3.377\ \times\ 10^{17}$$

a shorthand way of expressing the number of cubic miles that, as volume, the sun contains. We carried the mantissa (decimal portion) out to three places because it is untraditional to carry it out to more; too many numbers in the mantissa is regarded as unprofessional. Where more than three numbers appear in the expression unto which you are converting to scientific notation, round off to significant digits. For example, the number 2,578,621 may be written in scientific notation as 2.579×10^6, or further rounded to 2.58×10^6, indeed, ultimately to 2.6×10^6. Where the digit to the right of a number is equal to or greater than 5, simply increase the value of the number on the left by 1, and drop the one on the right. For example, 2,789 rounds off to 2,790, 378 to 380, etc. With comparatively little sacrifice of accuracy, we may round off our figure for solar volume to 3.38×10^{17}.

Now, let us turn to the use of scientific notation as it pertains to the writing of very small numbers. Recall the explanation regarding negative exponents, in which it was shown that a negative exponent exists as the reciprocal of its positive counterpart. (i.e., as $1000 = 10^3$, so $1/1,000 = 10^{-3}$). The reciprocal of a large number is always a small number. Since this is so, once again we need but multiply our negatively exponentiated base by some number, the result of which will be the number that we wish to express. We find that number, as well as the value of the exponent, simply by counting decimal places.

For example, let's take the number 0.00041, read as "forty-one hundred thousandths." In order to determine what the exponent should be, we shall begin with the decimal point, and count the number of decimal places preceeding the non-zero numbers. That is, we will add the number of zeros *and* the decimal point. Since there are three zeros, and 3 + 1 = 4, we shall write:

$$\times \ 10^{-4}$$

Now, we are faced with locating some number, which when multiplied by 10^{-4}, (1/10,000), will be equal to 41/100,000. We could proceed in the same manner as we did before, when working with positive exponents, in which we set up the question, ''what number, n, multiplied by 10^{-4} equals 41/100,000?'' in equation form, i.e.,

$$10^{-4} \cdot n \ = \ 41/100,000$$

which we subsequently divide,

$$\frac{41/100,000}{10^{-4}} = 4.1$$

revealing 4.1 to be our characteristic and mantissa. However, notice that 4.1 is simply the last part of the number we converted, the only difference being the insertion of a decimal point between the 4 and the 1. We have, it would seem, found a means by which to simplify our conversions. If we take such a number as 0.0000037, we may convert it if we:

(1) Determine the value of the exponent by counting zeros *starting with* the decimal point.
(2) Insert a decimal point between the non-zero numbers. This is equivalent to division by 10, made possible as it is multiples of ten with which we are working, since we are using a base ten system.

By step #1, we count six places. Hence,

$$10^{-6}$$

is our exponent. #2 provides for 3.7, which combined with the above, results in the expression

$$3.7 \times 10^{-6}.$$

We may now, with ease, convert such an intimidating number as

0.0000000000000000000000000000000000000000000021

via our "rules":

$$\#1 \text{ results in } 10^{-45}$$
$$\#2 \text{ results in } 2.1$$

providing for 2.1×10^{-45}, a considerably easier and less cumbersome manner in which to express the incredibly tiny number by which the volume of the proton is represented in cubic meters.

The zero that appears to the left of the decimal point, e.g., 0.000341, is not to be counted with the other zeros. Customarily, zero is used to preceed the decimal point in order to call attention *to* the decimal point. Apart from that, zero, in this context, has no further meaning.

Scientific notation is a quick and easy means to render large, or otherwise difficult numbers workable. It is a valuable and thoroughly engrained tool by which a great deal is simplified. To review, merely remember, when dealing with small number values, to count all the zeros and to include the decimal point in the count; divide the non-zero numbers by ten and, rounding off if necessary, set the result as your characteristic and mantissa. The same, only reverse somewhat, holds for large numbers. For example,

$$27,988,000$$

requires for conversion only that we insert a decimal point between the first and second numbers,

$$2.7988000$$

count the number of digits after the decimal point (in the case of large numbers, we do not include the decimal point in the count) and set your exponent equal in value to it: 10^7.

Setting the characteristic and mantissa against the base and exponent, we have, upon rounding,

$$2.799 \times 10^7.$$

That is all there is to it.

Now, with your knowledge of exponents, you are enabled to quickly and easily handle what appear to be rather large order calculations. For example, were you called upon to calculate (without benefit of a calculator) something on the order of

$$\frac{20,000 \times 5,000 \times 800}{400,000}$$

you would know at a glance that the problem could be rewritten as

$$\frac{2 \times 10^4 \cdot 5 \times 10^3 \cdot 8 \times 10^2}{4 \times 10^5}$$

and solved as easily as

$$\frac{2 \times 5 \times 8}{4} \times \frac{10^4 \times 10^3 \times 10^2}{10^5} = \frac{80}{4} \times \frac{10^9}{10^5} =$$

$$20 \times 10^{9-5} = 2.0 \times 10^5$$

EXERCISES

Express the following in scientific notation:

1. 200

2. 307

3. 2,756

4. 7,750,000

5. 0.00276

6. Show at least 3 ways in which 2,379 may be written.

Convert to scientific notation and compute, without the aid of a calculator:

7.

$$\frac{6,000 \times 4,000 \times 2,000}{2,400,000}$$

8. If $\pi \approx 3.14$, and $r \approx 4{,}000$, what is the approximate volume of the Earth, in cubic miles, where volume V is given by

$$V = \frac{4\pi r^3}{3}$$

7

Fractional
Exponential Notation

We've seen exponents of the type X^n, and even X^{-n}. However, to this point, we've encountered nothing on the order of $X^{n/m}$.

Such notation, an example of which is $10^{1/2}$ (read "ten to the one-half") is known as fractional exponential notation. It provides for a means whereby simplification may be made, easing and streamlining computation in virtually all areas and levels of mathematics. The principle upon which it is built is uncomplicated and straightforward, grounded in simple arithmetic. This becomes evident when we consider an expression of fractional notation, such as $x^{1/2}$, where x might represent any number. How would one go about multiplying such an expression by itself? Recall that, according to the rule dealing with the multiplication of exponents, $X^n \cdot X^m = X^{n+m}$. This being the case, then $X^{1/2} \cdot X^{1/2} = X^{1/2+1/2}$, or X^1. We know that any number raised to the first power is unaltered; hence, $X^1 = X$, testifying to the fact that the only number that can be multiplied by itself that will produce X is $X^{1/2}$. If $X^{1/2}$ times itself results in X, it must follow that $X^{1/2}$ is the *square root* of X. Such being so, we may pursue this line of reasoning yet further, and inquire as to if a similar situation evolves regarding $X^{1/3}$. Multiplication by itself twice only results in $X^{1/3+1/3} = X^{2/3}$. However, multiplication by itself three successive times results in $X^{1/3+1/3+1/3} = X^1$, or X, showing us that $X^{1/3}$ is the *third* or cube root of X. And so it goes . . . $X^{1/5}$, $X^{1/9}$, $X^{1/27}$, etc., being the fifth, ninth and twenty-seventh roots of X, respectively. Resultantly, we conclude that any root of a number may be designated, in general, by

$$X^{1/n}$$

where n is the root being represented. However, what of situations wherein the numerator of the fractional exponent is a number other than 1?

When we multiplied $X^{1/3+1/3}$, we received for our product, $X^{2/3}$. What is the significance of this expression?

The significance of fractional exponents may be summed thusly: The numerator of the fractional exponent is the power to which the base is brought, while the denominator of the fractional exponent is the *root* unto which it is lowered. Hence, $X^{2/3}$ is saying, "a number, x, brought to the second power, then taken to its third root." For example, if X were equal to 27, i.e., $27^{2/3}$, we would proceed first to take 27 to the second power, (square it) producing 729, which we would then take to the third root: 9. So, $27^{2/3} = 9$.

In non-exponential notation, the square root of a number is indicated via the symbol "$\sqrt{}$", known as a "radical," a word originating from the Latin word "radix," meaning, appropriately, "root." The square root of a number n is shown as $\sqrt{n}$. The third root is designated $\sqrt[3]{n}$, and so on, the superscripted number indicating the root involved. In designating the square root, however, one need not write $\sqrt[2]{n}$, as the absence of a superscript is universally taken to mean the square, or second root.

In radical notation, then, $27^{2/3}$ is written as

$$\sqrt[3]{27^2}$$

and says "twenty seven, squared, then taken to its third root:"

$$\sqrt[3]{27^2} = \sqrt[3]{729} = 9$$

Hence,

$$\sqrt[n]{x^m} = X^{m/n}$$

The process by which a number is raised to a power and then lowered to a root provides us with examples of those operations known as *involution*, the raising of a number to any power, and *evolution*, the extraction of a root from any given power.

We determined previously that negative exponents resulted in reciprocation of the number involved, i.e.,

$$X^{-n} = \frac{1}{X^n}$$

Nothing in this regard changes concerning fractional exponents:

$$X^{-n/m} = \frac{1}{X^{n/m}}$$

Consider $3^{1/3}$, a fractionally exponentiated expression, indicating the third root of three, which is approximately equal to 1.44.

Let us reciprocate that, i.e., $1/1.44$, (or 1.44^{-1}) obtaining, 0.694. Now, let us observe the result of setting our expression, $3^{1/3}$, unto a *negative* exponent of the same value, $3^{-1/3}$:

$$3^{-1/3} = 0.694.$$

So, we see that the reciprocal relationship indeed holds up for fractional exponents.

In general, then, we may define those operations associated with fractional exponents symbolically as

$$X^{(power/root)}$$

EXERCISES

A. Express the following in the form of fractional exponential notation:

1. $\sqrt{7}$

2. $\sqrt[3]{27}$

3. $\sqrt[4]{54^2}$

4. $\sqrt[5]{87^2}$

B. Write the following in radical nomination:

1. $3^{3/2}$

2. $X^{m/n}$

3. $52^{2/3}$

4. $(a \cdot b^3)^{1/2}$

C. Multiply the following:

1. $X^{3/2} \cdot X^{3/2}$

2. $m^2 \cdot m^{2/3}$

3. $N^{3/4} \cdot N^{5/6}$

D. Perform the following, as instructed:

1. Write the cube root of twenty-seven in fractional exponential notation.

2. Write the radical expression for the 4th root of sixty-seven, squared.

3. Express the value one twenty-seventh in exponential form.

4. Show the manner in which the reciprocal of the third root of five, squared, is written in fractional exponential form.

8
Logarithms

In having studied exponents, we have already begun a study of logarithms. A logarithm, by definition, *is* the exponent to which a particular base must be raised in order to achieve a desired number. This should serve to somewhat "demistify" logarithms; exponents *are* logarithms.

In the previous section, we determined that any number can be expressed as a power of ten. Since this is so, it follows that the powers of ten can be used in computations involving any number.

We saw, in scientific notation, that any number *greater than ten* can be expressed as a product of a number between one and ten, and a power of ten. That is, 2,000 can be expressed as the product of 2 and the third power of 10: 2×10^3. However, is it possible to express numbers *between* one and ten as a power of ten?

It was shown that $10^0 = 1$, and that $10^1 = 10$. Resultantly, we see that any number between one and ten that we would wish to express as a power of ten would require, for exponent, something between 0 and 1.

In about 1600, Scottish mathematician John Napier and English geometry professor Henry Briggs developed a table of logarithms which showed what those values between 0 and 1 were. A partial list of their work is found in Table 8-1.

Table 8-1

10^0 1	$10^{.301}$ 2	$10^{.477}$ 3	$10^{.602}$ 4	$10^{.699}$ 5
$10^{.788}$ 6	$10^{.845}$ 7	$10^{.903}$ 8	$10^{.954}$ 9	10^1 10

Just as, for example, 200 is equal to 2×10^2, we are able to see, as a result of the table, that $2 = 10^{.301}$, or that $8 = 10^{.903}$, which answers the question asked earlier regarding as to whether or not it is possible to express numbers between one and ten as powers of ten.

This discovery Napier and Briggs chose to call "logarithms," a word formed by fusing two Latin words: "log," meaning "proportion," defined as "the relation of one part to another, or to the whole, with respect to magnitude, quantity or degree." The second part of the word, "arithm," is the first six letters of the word "arithmetic," and means "number." Hence, in speaking of logarithms, we are speaking of the relation one part of a number to another, i.e., base and exponent, characteristic and mantissa, and of its result: the whole, the magnitude of the number, that these components work in concert to create.

The system of logarithms they created, dealing as it does with base ten only, has evolved to become known as the system of "common" logarithms. Today, however, any set of exponents used for computation is called a system of logarithms, and many exist. Even so, we shall concern ourselves only with common, or base ten logarithms.

Logarithmic notation differs somewhat from exponential notation. Using real numbers, we may, as an example, note that in exponential form, $8 = 2^3$. Expressed in logarithmic form, the foregoing is written $\log_2 8 = 3$, which literally says, "the logarithm (exponent, or power) of 2, in order to produce 8, is 3." We are told that in order to arrive at eight logarithmically, we must raise our base, in this instance, 2, to the third power. We may generically state the logarithmic format as

$$\log_{\text{base}} \text{Desired No.} = \text{Power}$$

Let us "translate" the exponential equation $4^3 = 64$ into logarithmic format. The base in this instance is 4, the "desired number" is 64, and the power is 3. Hence,

$$4^3 = 64 = \log_4 64 = 3$$

The rules pertaining to logarithms provide freedom to set an exponent to any base whatsoever, allowing us to obtain any number we may wish.

For example, let us imagine a situation in which it is desired to raise the number 5 the proper number of times as to get 35. Since we, at present, do not know what the logarithm required in order to accomplish that is, we will, for the time being, let "x" represent it: $5^x = 35$.

A calculator offers a decided advantage over cumbersome books of logarithmic tables. With yours standing by, we shall proceed.

We will begin, as always, by setting ourselves up a question, in the form of an equation. In writing:

$$\log 5 \cdot x = \log 35$$

we are saying "the logarithm of 5, multiplied by some number, x, equals the logarithm of 35." Now, via your calculator, determine the logarithm of 5, and that of 35. Having secured these numbers, (log 5 = 0.6990, log 35 = 1.5441) we may substitute them in our equation:

$$0.6990 \cdot x = 1.5441$$

Once again, needing to know what to multiply by, we need only "undo" the multiplication stated in our equation. Since 0.6990 is the number being multiplied by the as yet unknown value, we shall set it as our denominator:

$$x = \frac{1.5441}{0.6990} = 2.2091$$

Now we know the value of x in our equation, $5^x = 35$. Substituting,

$$5^{2.2091} = 35$$

Just as in the case of scientific notation, the whole number portion of the logarithm is referred to as the characteristic; the decimal portion as the mantissa. Consequently, in the above, "2" is the characteristic, with ".2091", the mantissa.

Obviously, the more decimal places employed, the greater the accuracy. Rounding off as we have, we've achieved a reasonable approximation.

The sequence of actions taken whereby we obtained our conclusion, may be arranged after the manner of an algorithm:

$$N^x = y$$

$$\log N \cdot X = \log y$$

$$X = \frac{\log y}{\log N}$$

where

N = the number acting as base
x = the logarithm being sought
y = the number you wish to obtain by raising N to the power x

Recall that we have determined that the exponent is the logarithm. In the expression $10^3 = 1,000$, 3 is the logarithm of 1,000. It follows, then, that 1,000 is the *anti-logarithm* of 3.

Logarithms are of extreme importance in virtually all facets of science. For example, in the study of chemistry, we learn that pH is defined as the logarithm of the reciprocal of the concentration of hydrogen ions (protons) in a solution. Hence, in determining the pH of 0.1 molar hydrochloric acid, we would proceed

$$\log 0.1^{-1} = 1$$

indicating a pH of 1; quite acidic indeed.

Water has a normal H^+ (hydrogen ion) concentration of 10^{-7} mol/litre, because of the slight ionization of water molecules. The pH is

$$\log (10^{-7})^{-1} = \log 10^7 = 7$$

indicating that water is neither acidic nor basic; it is neutral.

We are enabled to obtain, by way of brief examples, a glimpse of the importance of logarithms in helping to understand the world about us.

Learning the logarithmic function provides, at last, understanding of the reciprocal process, i.e.,

$$4^{-1} = 1/4$$

This is obviously an exponential equation which is saying that 4, raised to the negative first power, equals one-fourth. While this is true, the equation exists at the same time as the expression of reciprocal notation, saying that one-fourth equals the reciprocal of 4. Both statements are equally true. One is simply the other, inverted. *The inverse of an exponential function is a logarithmic function.*

"4⁻¹" provides an example of exponential notation. Inversion results in the advent of a logarithmic expression:

$$\log_4 \frac{1}{4} = -1$$

which is to say that the logarithm, or exponent, that four needs, in order to be brought to the value of one-fourth, is negative one.

This is, in essence, the reciprocal process, as taking any number to the power of negative one is equal to having divided 1 by that number:

$$X^{-1} = \frac{1}{X}$$

9
Computation Using Logarithms

Table 9-1

MULTIPLICATION OF LOGARITHMS

$$\log_b M \cdot N = \log_b M + \log_b N$$

DIVISION OF LOGARITHMS

$$\log_b \frac{M}{N} = \log_b M - \log_b N$$

MULTIPLICATION BY EXPONENTS

$$\log_b M^x = X \cdot \log_b M$$

These laws in Table 9-1 may be employed in ways that assist in the performance of routine calculations. For example, we may easily extract the square root of any number, using logarithms.

Example: Determine the square root of 64, logarithmically:

$$\sqrt{64} = 64^{1/2} = {}^1\!/_2 \cdot \log 64 = {}^1\!/_2 \cdot 1.8062 = 0.9031$$
Now, $10^{0.9031} = 8$

Example: Use logarithms to calculate

$$\frac{51 \cdot 4.1^2}{10.6} = x$$

x represents the as yet unknown answer. Proceeding,

$$\log x = \log 51 \cdot 4.1^2 - \log 10.6$$

$$= \log 51 + 2 \cdot \log 4.1 - \log 10.6$$

$$= 1.7076 + 1.2255 - 1.0253$$

$$= 1.9078$$

Now, $10^{1.9078} = 80.87 = x$

The first example was accomplished by way of the third property, regarding the multiplication of exponents, while the second example incorporated all three properties.

EXERCISES

Convert the following to logarithmic form:

1. $7^2 = 49$

2. $6.561 \times 10^3 = 9^4$

3. $0.4^2 = 0.16$

4. $4632.50 = 8.25^4$

5. $0.25^{0.75} = 0.35$

Solve the following equations, logarithmically:

1. $2^x = 8$ 2. $4^x = 27.25$

Answer the following questions:

1. What is the antilogarithm in the expression $12^2 = 144$?

2. What is the pH value for 0.5 molar HCL?

3. If the inverse of an exponential function is a logarithmic function, does it necessarily follow that a logarithmic function is the inverse of an exponential function?

Determine, logarithmically,

1. $\sqrt{36}$

2. $\sqrt{2}$

Use logarithms to compute

$$\frac{41 \cdot 16 \cdot 7.2^3}{11.4}$$

10
Fundamentals of Algebra

To this point, we've acquired familiarity with a host of elementary arithmatical concepts. Stopping for a moment, and, so to speak, looking behind us, we are able to see that many of the concepts involved emanate from predecessor concepts, themselves the off-spring of some progenitor, testifying unto the coherence, the consistency upon which our number system is built. This being so, it is only natural at this point to look ahead, anticipating the next step in the numerical and computational evolution of arithmetic: algebra.

If you are surprised to hear algebra described as an area of arithmetic, you are probably not alone. Many people mistakenly believe that algebra is the study of higher mathematics. It is not. It is *employed* in such studies, as algebra provides for an essential "streamlining," allowing us to do away with extraneous particulars, whereby we may set up equations, the result of which being that unknowns are replaced with solutions. In algebra, we are given means whereby we may cancel, reduce, and simplify. Indeed, it is from these very attributes that the name "algebra" originates.

About 825 A.D., an Arabian mathematician named Mohammed Ibn Musa Khowarizimi authored a book, which he titled *ilm al-jabr w'al Maqa balah*, which means the "science of cancellation and reduction."

As you might expect, Europeans found such a title difficult to pronounce. It underwent sufficient slurring until only one, rather distorted word of it was left: "aljabara." It is this word that eventually evolved into our word "algebra."

Algebra brings to us the power of the graph . . . literally, a picture of what the numbers are doing. This is of great assistance in a number of areas, as we shall see.

Among the greatest benefits associated with the use of algebra is the ability to work with unknowns, quantities possessing undetermined values. Such unknowns are represented by particular letters of the alphabet, an idea stemming from as long ago as about 1585, having originated with French mathematician Francois Vieta. For this reason, Vieta has been referred to as the "father of algebra."

A basic equation, containing one unknown, may be expressed, for example, as

$$x + 5 = 7$$

in which we are being told that a number, x, plus 5 equals 7. As a result of what we learned about negative numbers, we know that we can effect cancellation of the 5 on the left-hand side of the equation by adding −5 to it:

$$x + 5 + -5 = 7$$

This is the same as indicating

$$x + 5 - 5 = 7$$

resulting in

$$x = 7$$

However, in order to keep the equation in balance, we must do whatever we do to one side to the other as well. Hence,

$$x = 7 - 5$$

giving

$$x = 2$$

obviously, a solution to this simple equation.

The word "equation," as is evident in its spelling, is a means by which something is shown to equal, or be the same as, something else, i.e.,

$$7 + 2 = 3 + 3 + 3$$

Although it is expressed differently on both sides of the equals sign, the above says that "nine equals nine." We may do whatsoever we wish to one side of our equation, only as long as we make certain that we do exactly the same thing to the other side. In this way, the equation remains an *equation*:

$$2 \cdot (7 + 2) = (3 + 3 + 3) \cdot 2$$

The parenthesis, as used above, indicate that the numbers contained within them are to be taken as a whole. In this way, confusion is eliminated. For example, had we written

$$2 \cdot 7 + 2 = 3 + 3 + 3 \cdot 2$$

we would have wound up with

$$14 + 2 = 9 \cdot 2$$

which yields

$$16 = 18$$

obviously incorrect. Hence, we are led to see the importance of the use of parenthesis in algebra.

The use of parenthesis is governed by rules . . . rules by which ambiguity is removed, the result of which is that everyone who endeavors to communicate mathematically may be understood, regardless of the nation in which he may live, or what the language of that nation may be. All are enabled to come to the same conclusions.

When dealing with an expression containing many sets of parenthesis, or brackets, one is instructed to always start with the innermost set, and work outward.

For example,

$$10 + [3 + 7 + (2 - 1)]$$

is solved, first by

$$10 + [3 + 7 + (1)]$$

then

$$10 + [10 + 1] = 10 + 11 = 21$$

The second rule of parenthesis deals with signs, particularly that by which a negative number is designated, " – ". Anytime a set of parenthesis or brackets is preceeded by a negative sign, *all the signs of all numbers contained within the parenthesis or brackets are to be changed to their opposites upon removal of the parenthesis or brackets.* For example,

$$4 - (3 + 7 - 9)$$

becomes

$$4 - 3 - 7 + 9 = 3$$

A third use of parenthesis involves multiplication. Parenthesis, or brackets, as used in algebra, are another way of designating multiplication. Hence,

$$3(4) = 12$$

or,

$$2(5 - 2) = 2(3) = 6$$

Where it is required that many quantities be separated from one another, parenthesis and various brackets will be used:

$$7 \{2[(3 \cdot 2) - 7]\}$$

The order of operations does not change; begin working with the innermost set, and work progressively outward.

We may outline the rules associated with the use of parenthesis and brackets as follows:

1. Start with the innermost set, perform operations as indicated, and work outward.
2. When removing parenthesis or brackets that are preceeded by a negative sign, all signs of all numbers or terms contained within the parenthesis or brackets are to be opposited.

3. Parenthesis and brackets indicate multiplication.

Use these three guidelines to convince yourself that the example results in the answer −14.

EXERCISES

A. Solve the following simple equations by choosing the appropriate action to be taken on both sides of the equals sign.

1. x + 15 = 32

2. 7 + x = −9

3. 20 − x = −14

4. 120 · x = 314

5. 75 · x = 300

B. Use of parenthesis:

1. 2(6)

2. 5(15)

3. 200(4)

C. Solve the following:

1. 1 + [3 + (7 − 2)]

2. 7 − [4(2)]

3. 16 (32 − 9)

4. 5{−3[4(2 · 8)]}

5. 1 + {2[−3 − (6 + 2)]}

11
More Complex Equations

Although most of the computation that one is called upon to do throughout the course of daily affairs is of a rather simple nature, it is seldom so simple as to be handled entirely by the type of basic equation we have seen to this point. Up to now, we've seen the simplest of equations, ones in which a single, basic operation is sufficient to affect their solution. However, it is not at all uncommon to find many such operations required in order to solve a single equation. Nevertheless, this represents no difficulty. All the same rules apply; you simply proceed as the signs and symbols in the equation instruct. In order to facilitate our ability to solve any type of equation we might encounter, let us now learn a few more of the rules involved.

Throughout the course of this book, we have relied upon the dot ("$\cdot$") to indicate multiplication. In the section preceeding this one, it was explained that parenthesis or brackets mean multiplication as well; all numbers or terms contained within them are to be multiplied by the number immediately outside, unless another operation is indicated.

The conventions associated with the use of algebra account for yet another convenient way in which to indicate multiplication.

Consider the expression 3x. The "x" is the *variable*, as it can represent any number whatsoever; it may vary. The integer, (the "3"), is known as a "numerical coefficient," meaning that it works together with the variable. As 3 is unambiguously 3, that is, it does not change, the numerical coefficient is a *constant*.

Despite the fact that there is no multiplication dot between the coefficient and the variable, and neither is there a set of parenthesis involved, the manner in which the 3 and the x are situated relative to one another indicates multiplication. Whenever a coefficient and variable are so joined, i.e.,

$$2ab, \text{ or } 3xy \text{ or } 2a3cd,$$

multiplication is implied. *All* the terms of the expression are to be multiplied.

Example: Solve   2a3cd

where $a = 4, c = 6, d = 8$

$$2a3cd = 2 \cdot 4 \cdot 3 \cdot 6 \cdot 8 = 1,152$$

Example: Solve $3x[2y\ (7-2)]$

where $x = 3, y = 4$

$$3x[2y\ (7-2)] = 3 \cdot 3\ [2 \cdot 4\ (7-2)] = 9\ [8\ (5)] = 9 \cdot 40 = 360$$

Note that positioning the two numerical coefficients together does *not* indicate multiplication. If it were the case that it did, imagine the confusion that would result upon writing a simple double digit number, such as 64. No one would know if you mean to convey the quantity sixty-four, or if you mean six *times* four, or twenty-four. However, as already said, any number of variables (also called "literals") still implies multiplication, as this engenders no confusion.

Equations are designated by *order*. The order of the equation is equal to the value of the largest exponent it contains. For example,

$$x^2 + 7x + 12$$

is said to be a second degree equation, whereas

$$3x^3 + x^2 - 2x + 1$$

is classed as a third degree equation, or equation of the third order.

Now, let us consider the solution of equations only slightly more difficult. We shall solve:

$$2x + 3x + 4 - 2 = 21 - 3$$

an equation in which we note the presence of no less than three operations: multiplication, subtraction, and addition. This equation creates for us a good opportunity to provide ourselves with an example of what must first be done before solving any equation: group and calculate the similar terms.

Note that the equation contains a 2x term as well as a 3x term, connected with a plus sign, indicating that they are to be added. Each coefficient has an identical variable; one "x" cannot represent one quantity while another "x" stands for some other. All "x's" are equal, as are all "y's," etc. Resultantly, we may do as the sign connecting the two terms indicates, and add them: $2x + 3x = 5x$.

Of course, $4 - 2$ is 2, just as $21 - 3$ is 18. So, we may rewrite our equation as

$$5x + 2 = 18$$

a significantly less cumbersome expression.

Now, we have already seen that performing the same operation on both sides of the equals sign does not alter the equality; the equation remains an equation. Therefore, we may determine what the value of x must be if it is to be multiplied by 5, and have 2 added to it in order to equal 18. To find this value of x is to solve the equation.

$$5x + 2 = 18$$

$$5x + 2 - 2 = 18 - 2$$

$$5x = 16$$

$$x = {}^{16}/_5 = 3.2$$

Is our answer correct? There is really only one way in which to be absolutely certain. We will substitute our 3.2 value in place of x in the equation. If, as a result, it provides the answer 18, we will know that we are correct.

$$5 \,(3.2) + 2 \overset{?}{=} 18$$

$$16 + 2 \overset{?}{=} 18$$

$$18 = 18$$

There is a convenient method by which the solution of equations is expedited. It is called *transposition,* and involves, as its name implies, transposing, or moving, numbers.

As you may have noticed in the preceeding examples, the idea behind performing identical operations on both sides of the equals sign, apart from retaining the equality of the equation, is to isolate the variable being solved for. We want x set apart and alone; in maneuvering it to isolation, we may more easily solve for it.

Transposition offers a way to speed up this process. In transposing, we are free to simply pick up and put down terms on whatever side of the equals sign that is convenient. The only thing to bear in mind as we do, is that a term is to be changed to its opposite sign as it crosses the equals sign. For example, in the equation we just solved,

$$5x + 2 = 18$$

we may simply shift, transpose, the 2 on the left hand side over to the right, thereby placing the like terms together, remembering only to opposite its sign:

$$5x = 18 - 2$$

Now, upon subtracting, we are free to divide as we did before to obtain the value of x necessary to solve the equation.

EXERCISES

1. Determine 3xyz,

   where x = 2.3, y = 4, and z = 9.

2. Calculate 2nz,

   where n $\sqrt{2}$, z = − 1.

3. A number, situated along side a letter, is called a

   _____.

4. Letters, as used in algebra, represent _____.

5. Solve the following equations:

   (a) $7x[9y(z-3)]$ where $x = 2$, $y = 4$, $z = 7$.

   (b) $2x - 7 + (14z - 21c)$ where $x = 9$, $c = 30$, $z = 11.2$

6. $3x^4 + 2x^3 - 6x^2 + 2x - 2 = 0$
   is an example of an equation of the _____ degree.

7. Solve the following equations: (a) for x, (b) for c:

   (a) $6x + 2y - 4x + 5y + 2 = 3x - y + 2y - 6$

   (b) $4c + 7z - 9 = 9c - 31z + 5$

12
Graphing

At the beginning of this section, it was said that in algebra, we find the ability to graph, to see a picture of what the numbers are doing. This is one of the most helpful of all aspects of mathematics. By way of a graph, we are enabled to see at a glance how an equation responds as the result of substituting many different values for its variable.

It is the goal of science to provide understanding of physical phenomena, the world about us. In order for physical processes to be understood, they must be measured. We must be able to speak of "how much" or "how little," etc. In other words, we must be able to speak quantitatively. The language of quantification, or measurement, is mathematics, which, by way of its foremost tool, the graph, actually allows everything from otherwise invisible physical processes to be "viewed" (e.g., interactions on the subatomic level), to visible but otherwise difficult to understand realities, such as the behavior of an object under the influence of Earth's gravitational field.

The equation graphed is referred to as a *function*. A function is a relationship between two quantities such that one bears a direct influence upon the other; a change in one produces a change in the other. For example, you might consider the speed of your automobile as being directly dependent upon the amount by which the accelerator is depressed. Hence, your speed is a *function* of the degree to which your accelerator is depressed.

In the same way, when we graph an equation, we say that y is a function of x because y is totally dependent upon x. A different value of x will result in a different value of y in each case.

A function is designated by the notation "f (x)," and is read "f of x." Of course, a function may be denoted by any other variable. For example, a function more conveniently tagged "g" is written f (g), and pronounced accordingly.

The expression with which we worked in the previous section, 5x + 2 = 18, does not, as is, lend itself to graphing as it is solved for a definite value. Resultantly, x is constrained to remain one value only. However, should we transpose the 18, we may set the equation equal to zero,

$$5x - 16 = 0$$

a device by which we are enabled to graph. And since we will be graphing, our equation just became a function:

$$f(x) = 5x - 16$$

In order to graph, we will take a number line, turn it to right angles relative to the original, and join the two at zero:

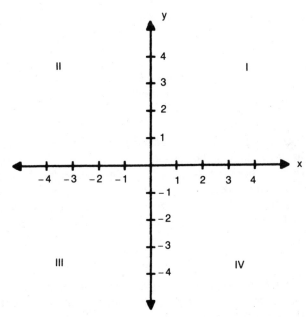

Fig. 12-1

Whereas the original number line was negative on the left and positive on the right, our new, intersecting number line is negative below and positive above. The horizontal line we designate "x." It is here that we will represent x values that we place into our function. The vertical line we correspondingly designate "y." It is here that we shall indicate the difference made by our function.

Together, the lines form what is called the "Cartesian coordinate axes," and provides means for graphing in two dimensions. The Roman numerals, circling counterclockwise about the coordinate system, designate the four "quadrants." Where the x and y axes meet is known as the "origin."

Let us now look to our function. We shall start with a number, a value of x, run it through our function, and see what we get for y. To start, let us run x = 1:

$$f(x) = 5x - 16 \text{ becomes } f(1) = 5(1) - 16$$

which is −11. Continuing sequentially to x = 6,

Table 12-1

x	y
1	−11
2	−6
3	−1
4	4
5	9
6	14

Table 12-1 depicts a particular value of x, and the result of running that value through the equation. As y is the function, the result of x, we could have just as easily labeled its column f(x).

We see, then, that when x = 1, y = −11, when x = 2, y = −6, and so on. These x,y values, seen together, are termed "ordered pairs," and are placed in parenthesis:

$$(x,y) = (x,f(x)) = (1,-11), (2,-6), \text{ etc.}$$

We are all set to graph. Taking our first ordered pair (1, −11), we locate 1 on the x axis, and, in line with it, locate −11 on the y axis. Here, we place a small dot:

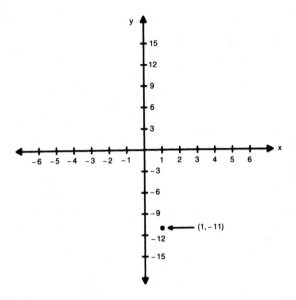

Fig. 12-2

This designates that when x = 1, y = −11. (The y axis has been scaled in increments of three in order to save space.) Continuing in the same fashion with the remaining sets of ordered pairs,

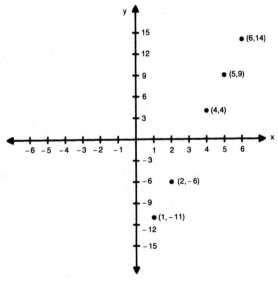

Fig. 12-3

Lastly, we simply connect the dots, forming a line, in essence, a picture of the equation:

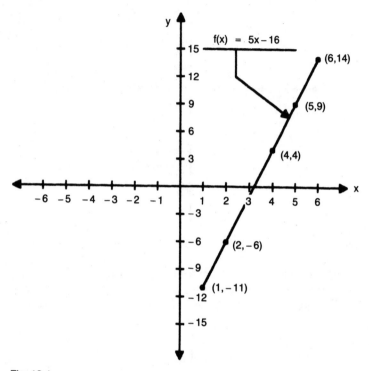

Fig. 12-4

Notice the line that constitutes the graph is straight. For this reason, functions of degree 1 are referred to as "linear functions." The point at which the line crosses the x axis is called the "x - intercept." It crosses the y axis, as one might expect, at the y - intercept.

Graphs of linear functions depict a constant rate of change in smooth, continuous fashion. A linear function may be used for the conveyance of information of such items that work in this manner. For example, the function by which degrees Celcius are converted to degrees Fahrenheit,

$$f(x) = {}^9\!/_5 x + 32$$

may be graphed in the same manner as the one we have done, showing the relationship between the two temperature scales:

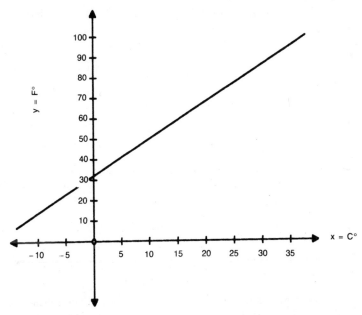

Fig. 12-5

We may see via a glance at the graph that 0° Celcius is the same as 32° Fahrenheit.

One of the greatest advantages offered by the mathematical reasoning process is the ability to extrapolate much information from comparatively little. To illustrate this, suppose we consider a vehicle, traveling at a constant speed of 30 miles per hour. In 60 minutes, the vehicle, of course, has travelled thirty miles. Since each mile is composed of 5,280 feet, in 60 minutes the vehicle has travelled $30 \times 5,280 = 158,400$ feet. As each hour is composed of 60 minutes, and each minute of 60 seconds, the vehicle is traveling at the rate of

$$\frac{158,400}{60^2} = 44 \text{ feet per second}$$

A similar argument will show that at 60 m.p.h., the vehicle covers 88 feet per second. Based on this information, how would you go about constructing a graph from which information could be readily obtained with regard as to what various mile per hour velocities equal in terms of feet travelled per second?

We may begin by constructing a standard set of x,y coordinates:

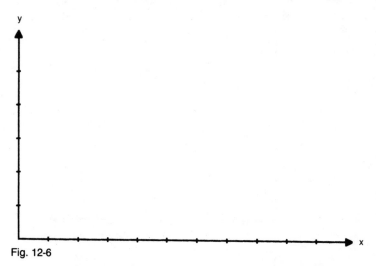

Fig. 12-6

Since it makes no sense to speak of speeds of automobiles as being less than zero, the negative portions of both the x and y axes have been omitted. We shall designate the x axis as speed in miles per hour, and the y axis as speed in feet per second:

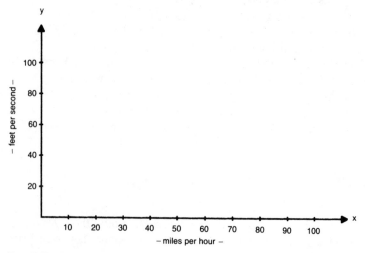

Fig. 12-7

At 30 m.p.h., we saw that the vehicle travelled at the rate of 44 feet per second, and at 60 miles per hour, 88 feet per second. Hence,

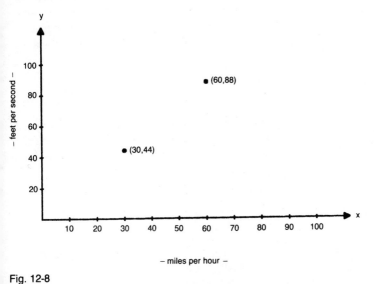

Fig. 12-8

Connecting the dots, we have our graph:

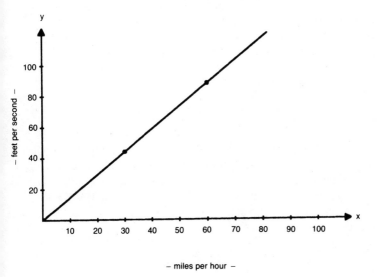

Fig. 12-9

73

We see that the line of the graph is representative of a linear equation, or function. We also see that it possesses a definite slope. If the slope were different, i.e., steeper or less sharp, it is easy to see that the relationship between miles per hour and feet per second would be affected. Obviously, then, the magnitude, or amount of slope is of great importance: *slope signifies the rate of change.*

Exactly what that rate of change is may be determined via

$$m = \frac{\Delta y}{\Delta x} = \frac{y_2 - y_1}{x_2 - x_1}$$

The "m" designates the slope, while the small triangle, Δ, actually the Greek letter "delta," is read as "change of." To determine the slope of the function, we may employ the ordered pairs that we used to graph:

$$m = \frac{\Delta y}{\Delta x} = \frac{88 - 44}{60 - 30} = \frac{44}{30} = \frac{22}{15}$$

Now we know the rate at which our function undergoes change; the slope value of our linear graph.

When we graphed $f(x) = 5x - 16$, we used the equation to determine the line of the graph. Now, using the ordered pairs in the manner that we have, as well as the value for slope, we may, conversely, determine the equation that corresponds to the line. This is accomplished via a formula:

$$y - y_1 = m(x - x_1)$$

All we need to do is substitute the values:

$$y - 44 = {}^{22}/_{15}(x - 30)$$

At the beginning of this book, we used the "partial product" method to multiply such problems as 83×8, in which we proceeded by writing 80 as $80 + 3$. We then multiplied both values by 8, and summed: $8(80 + 3) = 640 + 24$, or 664. We will proceed with the multiplication of the above expression, ${}^{22}/_{15}(x - 30)$, in the same manner:

$$y - 44 = {}^{22x}/_{15} - 44$$

Using our technique of transposition, we shall solve for y by moving the -44 from the left side to the right, remembering as we do to change its sign:

$$y = {}^{22x}/_{15} - 44 + 44$$

which yields

$$y = {}^{22x}/_{15}$$

Now we know the equation of the line, we have the function:

$$f(x) = {}^{22x}/_{15}$$

Knowing the function, we can instantly calculate what any mile per hour speed equals in feet per second. For example, 45 m.p.h. is equal to

$${}^{22x}/_{15} = {}^{22(45)}/_{15} = {}^{990}/_{15} = 66 \text{ ft./sec.}$$

Since ${}^{22}/_{15}$ times the x value gives that of the y, it follows that solving the function for y would produce the x coordinate. Starting with

$${}^{22x}/_{15} = y,$$

recalling that division is the inverse of multiplication, we use multiplication to "undo" the division. Since 22x divided by 15 equals y, it follows that y times 15 equals 22x:

$$15y = 22x$$

Dividing both sides by 22 will cause cancellation on the left, leaving the x:

$$\frac{15y}{22} = \frac{22x}{22} \text{ or } x = \frac{15y}{22}$$

In this case, the inverse of the function is equal to its reciprocal. With the function as we have it now, multiplying feet per second by ${}^{15}/_{22}$ will give miles per hour:

$${}^{15(44)}/_{22} = {}^{660}/_{22} = 30 \text{ m.p.h.}$$

The ability to determine the equation of a linear graph may prove useful in a number of areas. For example, in the chemistry laboratory, nitric and hydrochloric acids are used in considerable quantity. Could a graph be of assistance in their preparation?

We note that the algorithm (recipe) by which 1M nitric acid is made calls for 125 mls of concentrated acid to be mixed with 1,875 mls of deionized water. We may also note that 12M nitric is the result of mixing 1500 mls of concentrated acid with 500 mls of water. Since we are, in both cases, dealing with nitric acid, there must be a relationship, a correlation. Let us go about determining it.

We may begin by setting ourselves up coordinate axes. On the x axis, we shall indicate molarity value. On the y axis, millilitres of concentrated acid required for a particular molarity. For convenience, we will scale the y axis such that we need not make our graph excessively large, while slipping in an occasional "extra" y value for the sake of accuracy. (See Figs. 12-10 and 12-11.)

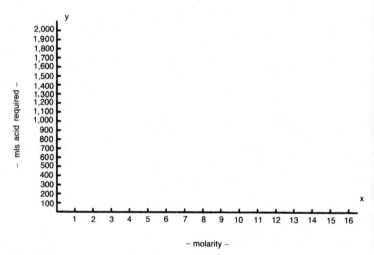

Fig. 12-10

Now, let us place and connect our points. 1M on the x-axis corresponds to 125 ml on the y-axis; 12M to 1500 ml.

Slope m is determined to be

$$m = \frac{y_2 - y_1}{x_2 - x_1} \quad \frac{1,500 - 125}{12 - 1} = \frac{1375}{11} = 125$$

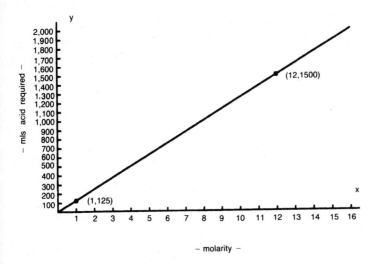

Fig. 12-11

Taking the formula for determining the equation of a line,

$$y - y_1 \quad m(x - x_1)$$

and substituting our x and y values, we conclude that

$$y - 125 = 125(x - 1)$$
$$y - 125 = 125x - 125$$
$$y = 125x - 125 + 125$$
$$y = 125x$$

is our function.

The number of millilitres required (y) is equal to the result of multiplying the desired molarity (x) by 125.

Notice, on the graph, that 2,000 mls of concentrated acid corresponds to 16M. We conclude that concentrated nitric acid is 16M in value.

EXERCISES

1. An equation into which certain values are substituted for the variable with the result being a change in another variable is called a _____.

2. A two dimensional graph is drawn on the _____ _____ system.

3. (x,y) is termed an _____.

4. Graph the linear function f(x) = 3x + 2.

5. If two molar HCL requires 344 mls of concentrated acid, and 8M HCL requires 1,376 mls concentrated acid, construct a graph whereby it can readily be seen as to how much concentrated acid is required for any molarity of HCL. What is the equation of the graph?

13
Higher Order Functions

Recall that in the last section, we performed multiplication of our line formula,

$$y - y_1 = m(x - x_1)$$

via the method learned in the first section of the book, called the "partial product method." A slight expansion upon this method results in the ability to multiply two expressions such as

$$(x + 3) (x + 4)$$

Starting with the first term in the left set of parenthesis, x, we multiply both terms of the second set of parenthesis:

$$(x + 3)(x + 4) = xx + 4x$$

Now, we repeat the process with the second term (3) of the first set of parenthesis:

$$(x + 3)(x + 4) = xx + 4x + 3x + 12$$

Since $xx = x^2$, and $4x + 3x = 7x$, the above expression may be written

$$(x + 3)(x + 4) = x^2 + 7x + 12$$

The manner in which we proceeded, multiplying from the first term of the left parenthesis to the outside term of the right parenthesis, then repeating with the inside term of the left parenthesis to both terms of the right parenthesis, begets an acronym, by which memory of the process is facilitated: *F*irst, *O*utside, *I*nside, *L*ast, or

F O I L

A variation of the method of partial products, the *FOIL* method, as used above, resulted in the creation of a second degree equation, known as a "quadratic."

"Quad" originates from the Latin word for "square." This is appropriate as the equation contains a second power or squared term.

Because any two numbers, when multiplied, result in a particular product, the two numbers are *factors* of that product. That is, the product is evenly divisible by its factors—not too surprising, in view of the reciprocal relationship multiplication and division have with each other.

As an example, suppose we multiply 3 and 7, the result of which being the product 21. Now, 21 is divisible by both 3 and 7.

Other products contain many factors; there is more than one set of two numbers which, when multiplied, result in that particular product. For example, 6 (2) = 12. However, 3 (4) also equals 12. Hence, we know that 12 is resolvable unto the factors 6,2,3 and 4; it is divisible by all four. It is therefore known as a "compound" number. Numbers that are divisible by no other numbers other than themselves and 1, such as 3, 7, 11, 13, etc., are known as *primes*.

As $(x + 3)$ and $(x + 4)$ result, when multiplied, in the expression $x^2 + 7x + 12$, we conclude that $(x + 3)$ and $(x + 4)$ are the *factors* of $x^2 + 7x + 12$.

An expression such as $(x + 3)$ is an example of what is called a "monomial." "Mon" originates from the Latin "mono," which means "one" (*mono*tone, *mono*rail), while "nomial" stems from the Latin "nomen," and means "name." A monomial is an expression of one part, requiring but one name.

$3x + 4y$ is an expression known as a "binomial," where "bi" means "two." (*Bi*cycle, *bi*lingual). Obviously, such expression as this contains two parts, two variables; two names are required.

A three term expression, such as $x^2 + 7x + 12$, is, as you might by now expect, a "trinomial." Expressions such as $2x^3 + x^2 - 3x + 1$, or $4x^5 - 6x^4 + x^3 - 2x^2 + 1$ are known as "polynomials." "Poly," again of Latin origin, means "many." Obviously, such expressions as third or fifth order equations require "many names" for their many parts. A trinomial, such as a quadratic, is usually referred to as a polynomial.

The quadratic equation is a most important tool in the understanding of physical phenomena. For example, ballistic motion within a gravitational field, (e.g., the motion of a cannonball) describes, throughout its journey, a path known as a "parabola:"

Fig. 13-1

What has a quadratic equation to do with the parabola? *When graphed, a quadratic equation inevitably produces a parabola.*

Any quadratic equation possesses the general form of

$$ax^2 + bx + c = 0$$

"a," "b," and "c" represent the numerical coefficients. In the event that one of the x's lacks a numerical coefficient, as in $x^2 + 2x - 4$, or $3x^2 + x + 1$, one is simply to consider that term to possess "1" for its coefficient. Any number multiplied by 1 is unchanged; the use of 1 as a coefficient where none otherwise exists helps in solving the equation. In $x^2 + 7x + 12$, a = 1, b = 7 and c = 12.

The standard form of the quadratic equation, $ax^2 + bx + c = 0$, may be algebraically rearranged such that x is isolated, hence solved for:

$$x = \frac{-b \pm \sqrt{b^2 - 4ac}}{2a}$$

Taking $x^2 + 7x + 12 = 0$ and transposing the c term, we get $x^2 + 7x = -12$, which tells us that there exists at least one number, such that it's square, when added to seven times itself, results in -12.

The standard form of the quadratic equation as solved for x, (referred to as the *quadratic formula*) as seen, provides the most expedient means by which to determine what the number or numbers may be. To locate these numbers is to solve the equation.

Let us determine the solution to the equation $x^2 + 7x = -12$. First, we'll affect re-transposition, and set our equation into the standard form:

$$x^2 + 7x + 12 = 0$$

As said, a = 1, b = 7 and c = 12. Resultantly, we need but insert these values into the formula

$$x = \frac{-b \pm \sqrt{b^2 - 4ac}}{2a}$$

as

$$x = \frac{-7 \pm \sqrt{7^2 - 4 \cdot 1 \cdot 12}}{2(1)}$$

Starting with the operations as called for under the radical,

$$x = \frac{-7 \pm \sqrt{49 - 48}}{2(1)}$$

which results in

$$x = \frac{-7 \pm \sqrt{1}}{2}$$

Just as $1^2 = 1$, so $\sqrt{1} = 1$. Hence, we have

$$x = \frac{-7 \pm 1}{2}$$

The "plus or minus" sign, ($\pm$) tells us, by its presence, that we are necessitated to perform two operations. We are told to add,

$$x = \frac{-7 + 1}{2} = \frac{-6}{2} = -3$$

As well as to subtract

$$x = \frac{-7 - 1}{2} = \frac{-8}{2} = -4$$

Resultantly, we have two answers, -3 and -4. Are these solutions to the equation $x^2 + 7x = -12$? Let's find out:

$$(-3)^2 + 7(-3) \overset{?}{=} -12$$

$$9 - 21 \overset{?}{=} -12$$

$$-12 = -12$$

Trying the next value,

$$(-4)^2 + 7(-4) \overset{?}{=} -12$$

$$16 - 28 \overset{?}{=} -12$$

$$-12 = -12$$

As there are two solutions, is there not the possibility that there might exist more? René Descartes, whom you may recall as the man for whom the Cartesian coordinate system was named, as well as he who invented exponents, postulated, in 1637, that every equation has as many solutions as it does orders of magnitude. That is, he believed, a second order (or degree) equation has two solutions, a third order, three, etc.

As it turned out, he was right, for in 1799, the German mathematician Carl Friedrich Gauss proved that any equation had, for solutions, a number equal in value to its highest exponent. No more, and equally important, no less.

Both of the values by which the equation is solved, -3 and -4, cause $x^2 + 7x + 12$ to equal zero:

$$x^2 + 7x + 12 \overset{?}{=} 0$$
$$(-3)^2 + 7(-3) + 12 \overset{?}{=} 0$$
$$9 - 21 + 12 \overset{?}{=} 0$$
$$0 = 0$$

You may easily convince yourself that the same is true when the value -4 is used.

If we take the zeros of our equation (also known as the *roots* of the equation), set them in parentheses with x's, and reverse their signs, i.e.,

$$(x + 3) \, (x + 4)$$

we have the *factors* of the equation, those values which, when multiplied, result in the advent of the equation itself. We see, then something very noteworthy here: *The factors of an equation are its roots, or zeros, with their signs opposited.* As a consequence, we may break most quadratic equations down to their component factors by use of the quadratic formula, the results of which to undergo sign reversal.

Notice that it was said that *most* quadratic equations could be so resolved. Consider such quadratic equation as $3x^2 - 9x + 14$. The quadratic formula, upon inserting the values, yields

$$x = \frac{-(-9) \pm \sqrt{-9^2 - 4 \cdot 3 \cdot 14}}{2(3)}$$

$$= \frac{9 \pm \sqrt{81 - 168}}{6}$$

$$= \frac{9 \pm \sqrt{-87}}{6}$$

Although we can square a negative number, we cannot take the square *root* of a negative number. The roots of such an equation are said to be "imaginary." This type of equation is not conventionally factorable.

Any number that is less than zero is, of course, a negative number, a concept, you may recall, that owes its popularity to Cardano, who, further, purposed to "invent" a number, the square root of which was -1. Such a number could not be found; it simply had no existence in the tangible, real world. It could only be *imagined*. Cardano therefore declared such number to be "imaginary."

About 1870, Swiss mathematician Leonhard Euler proposed that the symbol for the square root of -1 be a lowercase "i," for "imaginary." This suggestion gained universal acceptance, and is today the recognized symbol for $\sqrt{-1}$.

Just as -1 times any positive number results in that number becoming negative, while yet retaining its magnitude, so i times any square root results in that square root becoming negative. Resultantly, we may write

$$\frac{9 \pm \sqrt{-87}}{6} \text{ as } \frac{9 \pm i\sqrt{87}}{6}$$

a combination of real and imaginary numbers. In 1832, such combinations were labeled, by Gauss, as "complex numbers."

14
Graphing Quadratic Equations

We shall now tighten the scope of our concentration in regard to the quadratic formula. In particular, let us consider the set of terms found under the radical:

$$\sqrt{b^2 - 4ac}$$

This portion of the formula is known as the *discriminant*. It is here that the manner of root as possessed by whatever quadratic equation you are considering is determined. For example, in the event that performance of the operations it calls for result in 0, both of the roots are the same, equal.

Example: Determine the roots of the quadratic equation $3x^2 + 6x + 3$.

$$x = \frac{-b \pm \sqrt{b^2 - 4ac}}{2a}$$

$$= \frac{-6 \pm \sqrt{6^2 - 4 \cdot 3 \cdot 3}}{2(3)}$$

$$= \frac{-6 \pm \sqrt{36 - 36}}{6} = \frac{-6 \pm 0}{6}.$$

Now, $\dfrac{-6 + 0}{6} = -1$, and $\dfrac{-6 - 0}{6} = -1$.

So, although there are two roots, they are equal.

If the result of what transpires in the discriminant is greater than zero, as in the case of $x^2 + 7x + 12$, our first example, the roots are positive numbers; they are real and unequal.

When the discriminant produces a value less than zero, as it did when we solved $3x^2 - 9x + 14$, the roots are unequal and imaginary.

The discriminant reveals the nature of the roots, and the roots determine the manner in which the equation shall graph. It follows, then, that determining the roots of a quadratic equation assists in graphing it.

The graphing of a quadratic equation, or, for that matter any equation, is done in accordance with the point by point "connect the dots" method used in the graphing of linear equations. However, there are techniques by which graphing is greatly facilitated; some of which shall be explained as they pertain to quadratics.

To begin with, we shall construct a set of Cartesian coordinates, upon which we shall graph $x^2 + 7x + 12$.

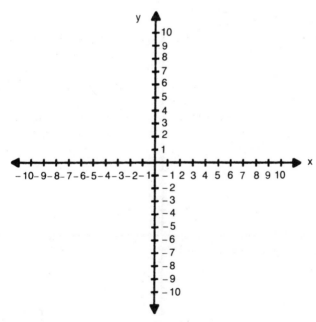

Fig. 14-1

Our next step is to run some numbers through the function. Starting with -5,

$$f(-5) = (-5)^2 + 7(-5) + 12 = 2$$

So, when $x = -5$, $y = 2$. Continuing, the following ordered pairs are obtained:

x	y
-5	2
-4	0
-3	0
-2	2
0	12
2	30

Now, the dots are placed upon the axes system . . .

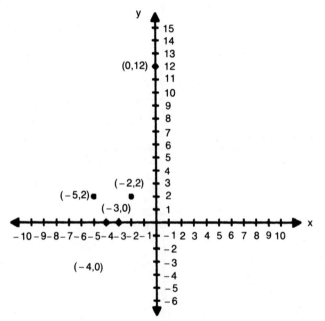

Fig. 14-2

Upon connecting the dots, we have our graph:

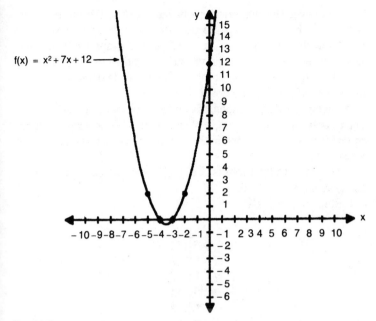

$f(x) = x^2 + 7x + 12$

Fig. 14-3

We are, at last, treated to a view of the parabola. Let us observe some of the features of this graph. Notice that the graph crosses the x-axis at x = −3 and at x = −4. At these values of x, y = 0. Recall that when we solved the equation $x^2 + 7x + 12$, it was these values we obtained for what was then termed the *zeros* of the equation. Now, you can easily see why such values are so designated. The *zeros* of an equation are those values of x at which y = 0.

Now, notice that the graph intercepts, or crosses, the y-axis upon our having run the value of ''0'' through the function, i.e., (0,12). Further, we observe that the value of c in this particular equation is also 12. We may also make note of the fact that the parabola opens upward, like a bowl of some sort, set right-side-up.

That running 0 through the function should produce the c value is not at all difficult to understand. Zero, squared, is still zero, and multiplying zero times seven, of course, yet results in zero. However, adding twelve and 0 produces twelve; telling us that the point at which the y-axis is crossed by the graph, known as the ''y-intercept,'' is given by running 0 through the function. Even more expedient is the realization that the y-intercept is equal to the c term of any quadratic equation.

Whenever the numerical coefficient holding the place of "a" (i.e., $ax^2 + bx + c = 0$) is positive, the parabola opens upward, as it does in the case of $x^2 + 7x + 12$, whose graph we have seen. However, where "a" is negative, such as in the case of $-3x^2 + 2x - 4$, the opposite situation occurs. The parabola opens downward, like a bowl turned upside down.

Having seen the graphs of equations possessing real and unequal roots, what of the graph of an equation possessing imaginary roots? Is there a difference in the manner in which such an equation would graph?

Most assuredly, there is. Let us determine that difference via the graphing of $3x^2 - 9x + 14$.

Running some x's,

x	y
−5	134
−3	68
−1	26
0	14
1	8
3	14

we get

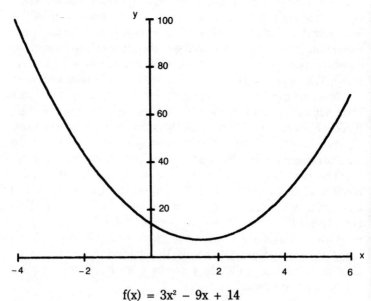

$$f(x) = 3x^2 - 9x + 14$$

Fig. 14-4

90

This graph at no point touches the x-axis. This equation and others like it, therefore *have no zeros*. Such functions are considered prime and unfactorable. That is why the quadratic formula, which we used on this equation, failed to resolve it to its zeros. It has none. Since zeros are factors with signs reversed, it follows that if the equation has no zeros, it has no factors.

So far, we have seen the graphs that result when the discriminant is greater than zero and less than zero. For the next example, we shall examine the situation involved when the discriminant equals zero, where we solved the equation $3x^2 + 6x + 3$. We found that this equation possessed identical roots. Via the graph, we shall see exactly what this means:

$$f(x) = 3x^2 + 6x + 3$$

x	y
−5	48
−3	12
−1	0
3	48
5	108

produces

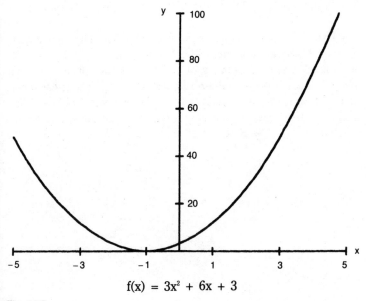

$$f(x) = 3x^2 + 6x + 3$$

Fig. 14-5

91

We are easily able to see that the graph of this equation inter-sects with the x-axis but once. It descends from the left unto -1, and then ascends, to the right, *from* -1. Since both roots, or zeros, are equal, we know that the factors are as well. Consequently, for factors we have

$$(x + 1) (x + 1)$$

a situation that is easy enough to verify. All one need do is multiply. If the function that we started out with results, our assertion will obviously be correct.

$$(x + 1) (x + 1) = x^2 + x + x + 1 = x^2 + 2x + 1$$

This isn't the equation! Must we recant our assertion regarding zeros and factors?

No. Despite the fact that at the moment it looks as though mul-tiplying the factors $(x + 1)$ and $(x + 1)$ has produced some other equation, in fact, it is the *same* equation. The numerical coefficients of the original expression have simply undergone the equivalent of having been divided by 3, a realization easily come to upon simple inspection of the result. We may easily affect restoration via:

$$3[(x + 1) (x + 1)] = 3[x^2 + 2x + 1] = 3x^2 + 6x + 3$$

That this is possible points to a particular fact: The equation $3x^2 + 6x + 3$ is an integral multiple of 3 in relation to $x^2 + 2x + 1$. As such, it possesses the same roots. Therefore, we conclude that an integral multiple of the numerical coefficients of a particular equa-tion possesses the same roots as the equation itself. Only the other x and y values change. To illustrate this, we shall superimpose the graph of $3x^2 + 6x + 3$ upon that of $x^2 + 2x + 1$:

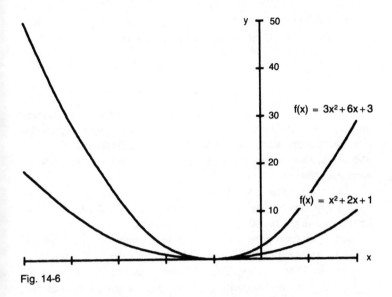

Fig. 14-6

We may significantly expedite the graphing of quadratic equations by acting upon a few of the observations made thus far, as well as incorporating some additional facts. Let us sum those observations, to this point, and posit those additionals.

1. The curve of which a quadratic, or second order equation shall consist, in every instance, is a parabola.
2. If "a" of $ax^2 + bx + c$ is positive, the parabola will open upward. If negative, the parabola will open downward.
3. The x intercepts (if any) will equal those values at which $ax^2 + bx + c = 0$.
4. The factors of the equation are the zeros of the function, with their signs reversed.
5. The highest (or lowest) point reached by the parabola is known as the *vertex*. The vertex, V, is given by

$$V = (x,y) = \left(\frac{-b}{2a}, \frac{4ac - b^2}{4a} \right) = \left(\frac{-b}{2a}, f\left(\frac{-b}{2a} \right) \right)$$

The x coordinate of the vertex results via $-b/2a$, the y coordinate as the result of the formula as seen occupying the "y" position of the ordered pair, or by running $-b/2a$ through the function.

6. An imaginary line by which the parabola is divided evenly at the vertex is called the *axis of symmetry*.

7. The y-intercept of the graph equals the c value of the function.

At the beginning of this section, it was said that the quadratic equation is instrumental in the understanding of physical phenomena, particularly, motion in a gravitational field. As an example of the use of the above expedients, let us see how the quadratic provides such information.

Let us imagine that an object has been launched into the air, ballistically. Since "ballistic" originates from the Greek word "ballein," meaning "to throw," we know that the object is not possessed of its own power, i.e., it has no engine, but must depend upon the force with which it is launched for all energy of motion, like a bullet fired from a gun. The question posed us is simple: If the object was launched straight up at the velocity of 400 feet per second, how long will it take to strike the ground, discounting air resistance?

We may begin by taking the standard form,

$$ax^2 + bx + c = 0$$

and inserting the proper values.

Experiment has shown that in the first second of fall, an object, descending freely in Earth's gravity, falls a distance of 16 feet. Since the object has been fired upward, Earth's gravity will, in this case, serve to act in such a way as to slow the object, ultimately stop it, then accelerate it back to the surface. We shall therefore represent the 16 ft./sec. value as negative, and insert it in place of "a" in the standard form:

$$-16x^2 + bx + c = 0$$

Since the velocity at launch is 400 ft./sec., we shall install this value as our second term, replacing "b":

$$-16x^2 + 400x + c = 0$$

There is no additional information; a "c" value is not necessary. Hence, we will consider it as possessing the value 0. Now,

$$x = \frac{-b \pm \sqrt{b^2 - 4ac}}{2a} = \frac{-400 \pm \sqrt{400^2 - (4 \cdot -16 \cdot 0)}}{2(-16)} =$$

$$\frac{-400 \pm \sqrt{160,000 - (0)}}{-32} = \frac{-400 \pm 400}{-32}$$

Now, $\frac{-400 + 400}{-32} = 0$, and $\frac{-400 - 400}{-32} = 25$

By #1 of the algorithm, we know that the graph of this equation will be a parabola. Via #2, we know that the parabola will open downward. By #3, we are informed that the parabola will intersect the x-axis at x = 0 and at x = 25; the zeros of the equation. By #5, the highest point of the parabola, (the vertex) will have for coordinates

$$V_{(x)} = \frac{-b}{2a} = \frac{-400}{2(-16)} = \frac{-400}{-32} = 12.5$$

$$V_{(y)} = f\left(\frac{-b}{2a}\right) = -16(12.5)^2 + 400(12.5)$$

$$= -2,500 + 5,000$$

$$= 2,500$$

The vertex occurs at (12.5, 2,500). #7 reveals that the parabola will cross the y-axis, since c = 0, at y = 0.

We now possess all the required information. All that is left to do is merely to set the points of our ordered pairs and connect the dots:

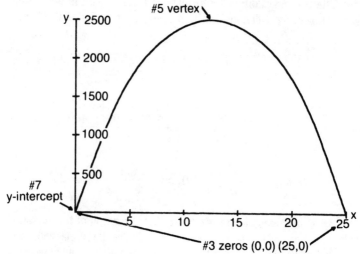

Fig. 14-7

What does this tell us? Quite a bit, for we see that the object will attain a maximum altitude of 2,500 feet in 12.5 seconds, after which it will fall for an additional 12.5 seconds, for a total flight time of 25 seconds, impacting the ground at a velocity of 400 feet per second.

Many examples of the usefulness of the parabola, the product of the quadratic equation, are to be found in science. Indeed, a relatively small amount of somewhat more advanced knowledge would allow us to extract considerably more information regarding the falling object, "pictured" above.

Despite the fact that we employed no concepts of an advanced nature, indeed, using only the essential basics of algebra, we were enabled to acquire a considerable amount of knowledge regarding the influence of gravity upon the planet whereupon we live. This testifies to the fact that algebra is indeed a most powerful and effective tool.

EXERCISES

1. Multiply the factors $(x + 2) (x + 5)$

2. What is the acronym of the method of multiplication used to multiply such expressions as the above? What does it stand for?

3. What is a second order equation commonly known as?

4. Provide an example of a fifth degree equation.

5. What is the standard form of the quadratic formula?

6. Write the standard form of the quadratic equation, (the quadratic formula) as solved for x, from memory.

7. How many roots does a second degree equation have?

8. What is the portion of the quadratic formula found under the radical known as?

9. Graph the following equations:
   (a) $x^2 + 7x + 10$
   (b) $x^2 + 6x + 4$
   (c) $(2x - 1) (x - 3)$

10. When the graph of the equation does not cross the x axis, its roots are said to be _____.

11. An object is fired from the ground, ballistically, at a velocity of 200 ft./sec. Discounting air resistance, determine
    (a) How long it will take to reach maximum altitude.
    (b) Maximum altitude.
    (c) Total flight time.

15
Polynomials of Varying Powers

We have seen the "partial product" method used at various times throughout this book, in which each term of an expression such as (a + b) was dealt with separately. Because the raising of numbers to various powers involves multiplication (e.g., $2^3 = 2 \cdot 2 \cdot 2$), it is natural to wonder if the same operative logic holds when raising monomials to powers. For example, does

$$(a + b)^2 = a^2 + b^2 \ ?$$

While the above might look reasonable, it is, in fact, incorrect. The proper result is:

$$(a + b)^2 = a^2 + 2ab + b^2$$

Where does the middle term come from? What is responsible for its creation, and, is it truly necessary? If so, why?

These questions may best be answered by means of an example. Consider a plot of land, square in shape, 50 ft. by 50 ft. Desiring to know the amount of square footage, or area, of the plot, one need but multiply 50 × 50, as Area = (Length · width), both of which, in this case, are equal. It is easily determined that the plot possesses 2,500 square feet of surface area.

Let us now complicate the matter somewhat. We shall consider the land as having been purchased by four investors. With the exception of two persons, the investors have purchased uneven allotments of the plot. The area owned by investor #1 is quite large, while that of investor #4 is rather small. Investors #2 and #3 possess strips of equal size.

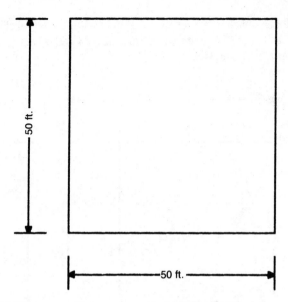

Fig. 15-1

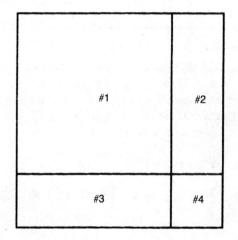

Fig. 15-2

We shall designate investor #1 as having land that is ''a'' units wide, and, being square, ''a'' units long. Because investor #2's land is equal in length to investor #1's, investor #2's land is also ''a'' units long, as is that of investor #3. However, investor #2's portion is obviously much narrower than that of investor #1. We shall designate it as being "b" units wide. Investors #3 and #4 also possess portions "b" units wide.

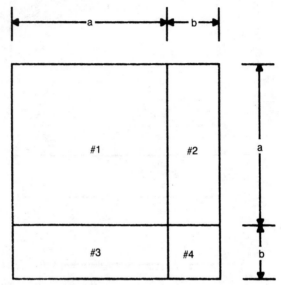

Fig. 15-3

It is apparent that the overall area of the land square will be equal to the sum of the areas owned by all four investors.

The diagram reveals the overall plot to have for length the value $(a + b)$, and for width, the value $(a + b)$ as well. Since, as we know, $A = Lw$, then $A = (a + b) (a + b)$:

$$(a + b) (a + b) = a^2 + ab + ab + b^2$$

Since $(a + b) (a + b) = (a + b)^2$, and $ab + ab = 2ab$, we may write

$$(a + b)^2 = a^2 + 2ab + b^2$$

this time with the understanding as to where the "mysterious" middle term came from.

By squaring $(a + b)$ incorrectly, as in the case of $(a + b)^2 = a^2 + b^2$, we have left out some vital information. To further help see this, consider our plot of land as possessing the following measurements:

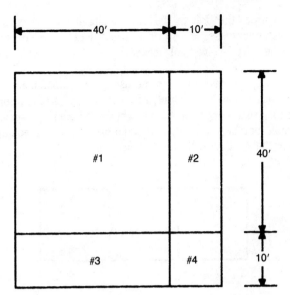

Fig. 15-4

We have let a = 40 ft. and b = 10 ft., for a total of 50 ft. by 50 ft., values that we know will produce 2,500 ft.^{2}

Now, using

$$(a + b)^2 = a^2 + b^2,$$

we get

$$40^2 + 10^2 = 1,600 + 100 = 1,700 \text{ ft.}^2$$

a figure that we know to be wrong. However, employing the *correct* expansion,

$$(a + b)^2 = a^2 + 2ab + b^2$$

we get

$$40^2 + 2 \cdot 40 \cdot 10 + 10^2 = 1,600 + 800 + 100 = 2,500 \text{ ft.}^2$$

the correct answer.

The seeming ''mathematical abstraction'' known as squaring, has a most definite real world counterpart. To square a figure is to elevate it from the first to the second dimension. As ours, to all physical appearances, is a world of three dimensions, we find real world tangibility involved not only with squaring, but with cubing as well.

Squaring, as said, involves the use of two dimensions, specifically, length and width. Multiplying a number by itself is referred to as squaring that number, as the ancient Pythagoreans observed that any whole number so multiplied could be drawn as a square. For example, let us start with three identical boxes:

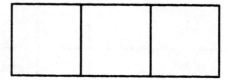

Fig. 15-5

Multiplying 3×3 results in the creation of nine boxes, three per side, creating an overall square,

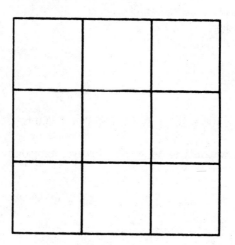

Fig. 15-6

showing the number 9 to be what is referred to as a "perfect square."

As said, ours is a world of three dimensions. We live in a world of not only length and width, but height as well. Taking our 3 to the third power, or *cubing* it, we find

$$3^3 = 27$$

providing geometrically for

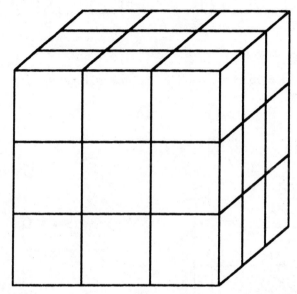

Fig. 15-7

a three dimensional square, otherwise known as a cube, consisting of 27 sub-cubes.

In similar fashion, a one dimensional monomial raised to the third dimension, $(a + b)^3$, also has real world tangibility.

Just as the above cube is actually the square, elevated to the third dimension, where it now possesses volume, so $(a + b)^3$ is $(a + b)^2$ raised to the third dimension, where it, too, now possesses volume:

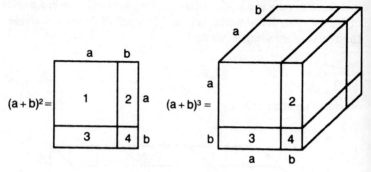

Fig. 15-8

If we were to take the three dimensional construct, and "blow it apart," i.e.,

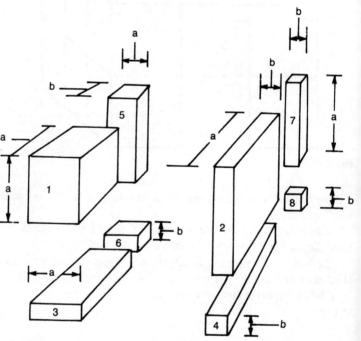

Fig. 15-9

we may clearly see that the volume of the overall solid will be equal to the sum of the volumes of its individual components, of which there are eight.

Total Volume = {(vol. seg. #1) + (vol. seg. #2) + . . . + (vol. seg. #7) + (vol. seg. #8)}

Just as A = LW, so V + LWH, adding the three dimensional quality of height. Looking at the diagram of the exploded solid, we see that component (or segment) #1 has, for volume,

$$aaa = a^3$$

Continuing,

> segment #2 has, for volume, aab = a^2b.
> segment #3 has, for volume, aab = a^2b
> segment #4 has, for volume, abb = ab^2
> segment #5 has, for volume, aab = a^2b
> segment #6 has, for volume, abb = ab^2
> segment #7 has, for volume, abb = ab^2
> segment #8 has, for volume, bbb = b^3.

Grouping the like terms gives

$$a^3 + a^2b + a^2b + a^2b + ab^2 + ab^2 + ab^2 + b^3$$

which is the same as

$$a^3 + 3a^2b + 3ab^2 + b^3$$

and provides for the volume of the solid.

Just as $2^3 = 2 \cdot 2 \cdot 2 = 4 \cdot 2$, so

$$(a + b)^3 = (a + b) (a^2 + 2ab + b^2)$$

$$= a^3 + 2a^2b + ab^2 + a^2b + 2ab^2 + b^3$$

$$= a^3 + 2a^2b + a^2b + 2ab^2 + ab^2 + b^3$$

$$= a^3 + 3a^2b + 3ab^2 + b^3$$

results that we may compare to those obtained by summing the volumes of the three dimensional construct into which this polynomial geometrically translates.

It seems likely that the next question a person would ask, having seen the real world counterpart of the squared monomial, and then that of the cubed monomial, is what its *fourth* dimensional counterpart looks like. Unfortunately, the concept of the fourth dimension is an exceedingly difficult one, mathematically, and since we cannot directly envision four dimensions, ours being a world of three, we are constrained to accept mathematical "pictures" only. Does this mean that polynomials cannot exist beyond those of the third order?

Of course not. An algebraic expression, such as the monomial we've been working with up to this point, can be raised to any power whatsoever, just as any number may be. The raising of polynomials to various powers is accomplished via a mathematical schema originated by Isaac Newton, known as the "binomial theorem." Use of the binomial theorem generates a group of numbers, which have come to be known as "Pascal's triangle:"

```
    0           1
  1           1 1
  2          1 2 1
  3         1 3 3 1
  4        1 4 6 4 1
  5      1 5 10 10 5 1
```

The numbers, as they run from left to right, are the numerical coefficients of polynomials as raised to the powers zero through five, represented by the string of numbers on the left. Starting from the top of the triangle and working down, "1" represents the numerical coefficient of a binomial raised to the zero power. (Recall that any number raised to the zero power is equal to 1.) Notice the coefficients of the second power. They are indeed the same ones employed in the expanding of $(a + b)^2$ into $a^2 + 2ab + b^2$, just as the third power coefficients, 1,3,3,1, are those used in the expansion of $(a + b)^3$ into $a^3 + 3a^2b + 3ab^2 + b^3$.

Notice the exponents in the above expansions. Each term of each expression contains exponents that sum to the value of the power of the expression. For example, in the above third power expression, "a" has an exponent of 3, with the following term possessing "a" to the second power, coupled with "b" to the first, for a total of three. Observe further that the exponent of "a" decreases left to right, while that of "b" increases.

Pascal's triangle provides considerable ease in raising polynomials to virtually any power. As an example of its use, we shall raise $(a + b)$ to the fourth power:

$$(a + b)^4 = a^4 + 4a^3b + 6a^2b^2 + 4ab^3 + b^4$$

We simply insert the coefficients, and alter the size of the exponents across the expression in the manner pointed out above. Follow this format when raising a binomial to any specified power. For your assistance, there is an expanded version of Pascal's triangle provided in Appendix C of this book.

EXERCISES

Expand the following monomials

1. $(d + e)^2$

2. $(c + d)^3$

3. If a cube is a three dimensional square, what would a circle be in three dimensions?

4. Write the expansion for $(n + m)$ as a fourth degree polynomial.

5. Why doesn't $(a + b)^2 = a^2 + b^2$? Can you advance an argument as to why it doesn't work using integers (whole numbers) in place of "a" and "b"?

16
Manipulation of Equations

The degree of usefulness that an equation or formula may provide is often dependent upon the skill of its user to rearrange and manipulate it in such a way as to enable it to be of the greatest possible value. The most useful formula available unto whatever be the task at hand is little more than just so many terms set together, unable to benefit one who is incapable of the necessary manipulations whereby the formula is made to work.

We have seen a host of operations, rules, and guidelines whereby equations are rearranged. We have altered equations without damaging their equality, by adding, subtracting, dividing, multiplying, and transposing. We've learned the rules involving the use of signed numbers and their roles in equations. We've seen variables substituted and solved for, and have witnessed the usefulness of factoring and graphing. At this point, it seems appropriate to ask what the *practical* uses associated with the solution of equations may be.

This question may best be answered by way of an example. Imagine that you are assigned to the preparation of various molarity reagents. You have prepared 2 litres of 0.5^M hydrochloric acid. However, titration reveals the acid to in fact be 0.37^M, too weak to be of value. What do you do? Obviously, the preparation requires an additional amount of concentrated acid. But how much?

The answer is obtained via the use of the HCl "renormalization" formula:

$$(2,0000\delta) - 2000C = (-12x + Cx)$$

where

δ = titrated molarity, which is less than the desired value.

C = what the molarity should be.

The acid titrated at 0.37^M, despite the attempt to produce 0.5^M. Substituting these values, the formula

$$(2,000\delta) - 2000C = (-12x + Cx)$$

becomes

$$(2,000 \cdot 0.37) - 2,000 \cdot 0.5 = (-12x + 0.5x)$$

Remember, operations within parenthesis are performed first:

$$(740) - 2,000 \cdot 0.5 = -11.5x$$

$$740 - 1,000 = -11.5x$$

$$-260 = -11.5x$$

Now, recall that a negative divided by another negative produces a positive. That being so, we may proceed

$$-260/-11.5 = x$$

Or, we may stop to recall that transposition results in the sign of the term undergoing change to its opposite. That being so, we may simply have each term of:

$$-260 = -11.5x$$

trade places with one another, producing

$$11.5x = 260$$

which gives

$$x = {}^{260}/_{11.5} = 22.6 \approx 23$$

As a result of substituting variables, the use of signed numbers and division . . . in short, some of the skills whereby equations are manipulated . . . we know that adding 23 millilitres of concentrated acid to our 0.37^M HCl preparation will result in the obtainment of the value we seek.

We may also call upon algebra to bail us out of the opposite situation. Let us consider that we have inadvertently made the acid too strong. How much water should be added?

The formula:

$$\frac{(2,000\delta) - 2,000C}{C} = \text{mls H}_2\text{O}]$$

where

δ = titrated molarity of acid, being greater than that which is desired

C = what the molarity should be

answers that question.

To see how, let us imagine that our attempt at 0.5^M HCl resulted in the creation of 0.6. The amount of water required to dilute the mixture to 0.5^M is

$$\frac{(2,000 \cdot 0.6) - 2,000 \cdot 0.5}{0.5} = \text{mls H}_2\text{O}$$

$$\frac{1,200 - 1,000}{0.5} = \text{mls H}_2\text{O}$$

$$\frac{200}{0.5} = 400 \text{ mls H}_2\text{O}$$

Speaking of manipulations, a few upon

$$(2,000\delta) - 2000C = (-12x + Cx)$$

along with some slight alterations, results in

$$(\delta V) - (Vc) = -16x + Cx,$$

a formula whereby one molarity of nitric acid may be changed to another. Let us, in order to see it operate, now imagine that we have 30 mls of 8^M nitric, which we wish to convert to 12^M. How much concentrated acid is required?

In the formula:

$$\delta = \text{molarity of original acid, what you are working with}$$
$$V = \text{volume}$$
$$C = \text{desired molarity}$$

Now,

$$(\delta V) - (Vc) = -16x + Cx$$

$$(8 \cdot 30) - (30 \cdot 12) = -16x + 12x$$

$$240 - 360 = -4x$$

$$4x = 120$$

$$x = {}^{120}/_4 = 30 \text{ mls conc. acid}$$

These few examples serve to illustrate, in at least one area, the usefulness a knowledge of basic algebra can provide. The ability to set up and solve equations for particular variables empowers you to move quickly and accurately through the calculations whereby seemingly difficult problems are transformed easily into usable solutions. You now have a respectable arsenal of mathematical weapons at your command. Use them to your advantage.

EXERCISES

1. You have attempted to batch 2 litres of 8^M HCl. However, titration reveals that you have, instead, made 7.2 molar. How much concentrated acid do you need in order to bring the mixture to the proper molarity?

2. There is a 50 ml volume of 4^M nitric acid that you wish to convert to 7.3^M. Use

$$(\delta V) - (VC) = -16x + Cx$$

where δ = original molarity value, V = volume and C = desired molarity, to determine how much concentrated nitric is required.

3. It is necessary to turn a 30 millilitre volume of 4^M nitric acid into 8^M. How much acid is required?

4. Solve $ab + c = -3$ for "a."

5. The formula $C = 2\pi r$ describes any circle, and indicates that a circle's circumference is equal to 2π times the circle's radius. Solve the formula for radius.

Appendix A
The Greek Alphabet

A	α	alpha		N	ν	nu
B	β	beta		Ξ	ξ	xi
Γ	γ	gamma		O	o	omicron
Δ	δ	delta		Π	π	pi
E	ϵ	epsilon		P	ϱ	rho
Z	ζ	zeta		Σ	σ	sigma
H	η	eta		T	τ	tau
Θ	θ	theta		Υ	υ	upsilon
I	ι	iota		Φ	ϕ	phi
K	$\varkappa$	kappa		X	χ	chi
Λ	λ	lambda		Ψ	ψ	psi
M	μ	mu		Ω	ω	omega

Appendix B
Mathematical
Symbols

>	is greater than
>>	is much greater than
<	is less than
<<	is much less than
≤	is less than or equal to
≥	is greater than or equal to
=	equals
≠	does not equal
≈	approximately equals
±	plus or minus
∴	therefore
ϵ	is an element of the set
$\notin$	is not an element of the set
$\sqrt{}$	square root
$\int$	integral
Σ	(sigma) summation notation
:	is to, the ratio of
;	such that
α	is proportional to
≡	is identical to, is congruent to
∞	infinity (called the "lemniscate")
!	factorial (i.e., $5! = 1 \times 2 \times 3 \times 4 \times 5 = 120$)
f(x)	function notation
f'(x)	first derivative

Appendix C
Pascal's Triangle

POWER

0	1
1	1 1
2	1 2 1
3	1 3 3 1
4	1 4 6 4 1
5	1 5 10 10 5 1
6	1 6 15 20 15 6 20 1
7	1 7 21 35 35 21 7 1
8	1 8 28 56 70 56 28 8 1

Appendix D
Formulas
from Geometry

The Circle: $A = \pi r^2$

$\qquad$ $C = 2\pi r$ (C = Circumference)

Area of a triangle: $A = {}^{bh}/_2$ (b = base, h = height)

Hypotenuse of a right triangle: $c^2 = a^2 + b^2$.

Pyramid: $V = {}^{bh}/_3$ (V = volume)

Cone: $V = \dfrac{\pi r^2 h}{3}$

Sphere: Surface Area = $4\pi r^2$.   (r = radius)

$\qquad\qquad V = \dfrac{4\pi r^3}{3}$

Cylinder: $V = \pi r^2 H$ (h = height)

$\qquad$ Surface Area = $\pi r \sqrt{(r^2 + h^2)}$

Rectangle: $A = LW$ (L = length, W = width)

Answers to Exercises

PARTIAL PRODUCT METHOD

1. $3 \times 15 = 45$, and there are 3 zeros: 45,000.

2. $3 \times 3 = 9$, three zeros: 9,000.

3. $25 \times 50 = (20 + 5) \cdot 50$. $5 \times 2 = 10$, there are two zeros: 1,000. $5 \times 5 = 25$, there is one zero: 250. $1,000 + 250 = 1,250$.

4. $72 \times 1,000 = (70 + 2) \cdot 1,000$. $7 \times 1 = 7$, there are four zeros: 70,000. $1 \times 2 = 2$, three zeros: 2,000. $70,000 + 2,000 = 72,000$.

5. $302 \times 500 = (300 + 2) \cdot 500$. $3 \times 5 = 15$, four zeros: 150,000. $2 \times 5 = 10$, two zeros: 1,000. $150,000 + 1,000 = 151,000$.

6. $130 \times 100 = (100 + 30) \cdot 100$. $1 \times 1 = 1$, four zeros: 10,000. $1 \times 3 = 3$, three zeros: 3,000. $10,000 + 3,000 = 13,000$.

FRACTIONS

ADDITION
1. $2/3$ 2. $4/7$ 3. $27/20$ 4. $106/45$ 5. $169/176$

SUBTRACTION
1. $1/2$ 2. $3/7$ 3. $32/99$ 4. $4/65$ 5. $25/2414$

MULTIPLICATION
1. $7/20$ 2. $10/21$ 3. $765/806$ 4. $75/141$ 5. $144/1189$

DIVISION
1. $10/9$ 2. $8/9$ 3. $627/2$

REDUCING
1. $1/3$ 2. $3/4$ 3. $1/2$ 4. $1/3$ 5. $1/2$

PERCENTAGES

1. $3\% = 3/100 = 0.03$.

2. $0.05 \cdot \$50.00 = \$2.50$.

3. $6^{2}/_{3}$

4. $0.15 \cdot x = 30.\ x = 200$.

5. $0.07 \cdot 200 = \$14.00$ more.

6. $0.12 \cdot x = 2.50.\ x = \$20.83$.

7. Personnel distribution chart:

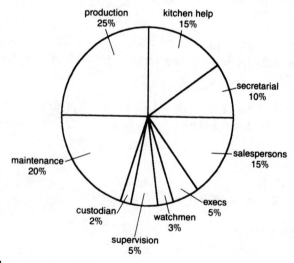

Fig. A-1

8. 70 production workers. 14 executives.

RECIPROCALS

1. $1/3$ or 3^{-1}.

2. $1/64$ or 64^{-1}.

3. $7/3$

4. b/a

5. $27/1 = 27$.

6. $3b/a$.

SCIENTIFIC NOTATION

1. 2.0×10^2 or 2×10^2.

2. 3.07×10^2.

3. 2.756×10^3.

4. 7.750×10^6.

5. 2.76×10^{-3}.

6. 2.739×10^3 or 27.39×10^2 or 0.2739×10^4. There are a number of ways in which the expression may be written; perhaps you wrote something not shown here. Does what you wrote equal 2,739? If so, you are correct.

7.

$$\frac{6 \times 10^3 \cdot 4 \times 10^3 \cdot 2 \times 10^3}{2.4 \times 10^6} = \frac{6 \cdot 4 \cdot 2}{2.4} \times 10^{3+3+3-6}$$

$$20 \times 10^{9-6} = 2.0 \times 10^4$$

8.

$$\frac{4\pi(4\times10^3)^3}{3} = \frac{4\pi(6.4 \times 10^{10})}{3} = 2.68 \times 10^{11} \text{ mi.}^3$$

FRACTIONAL EXPONENTIAL NOTATION & THE RADICAL

A.
1. $7^{1/2}$
2. $27^{1/3}$
3. $54^{2/4} = 54^{1/2}$
4. $87^{2/5}$

B.
1. $3^{3/2} = \sqrt{3^3}$
2. $X^{m/n} = \sqrt[n]{X^m}$
3. $52^{2/3} = \sqrt[3]{52^2}$
4. $(a \cdot b^3)^{1/2} = \sqrt{a \cdot b^3}$

C.
1. x^3
2. $M^{8/3}$
3. $N^{19/12}$

D.
1. $27^{1/3}$
2. $\sqrt[4]{67^2}$
3. 27^{-1}
4. $(1/5^{1/3})^2 =$
   $(5^{-1/3})^2 = 5^{-2/3}$

LOGARITHMS

a.
1. $\log 49_7 = 2$

2. $\log 6.651 \times 10^3{}_9 = 4$

3. $\log 0.16_{0.4} = 2$

4. $\log 4632.50_{8.25} = 4$

5. $\log 0.35_{0.25} = 0.75$

b.
1. $x = 3$

2. $x = 2.3841$

c.
1. 144

2. $\log 2$

3. yes.

d.
1. $\sqrt{36} = 36^{1/2} = 1/2 \cdot \log 36 = 0.77815125.$
   $10^{0.77815125} = 6.$

2. $10^{0.1505} = 1.414$
   $x = \log 41 + \log 16 + 3 \cdot (\log 7.2) - \log 11.4$
   $= 1.6128 + 1.20412 + 2.571998 - 1.056905$
   $= 4.331997.$
   $= 10^{4.331997} = 21,478.13$

ALGEBRA

A.
1. $x + 15 = 32.$ $-15 + 15 + x = 32 - 15.$ $x = 17.$

2. $7 + x = -9.$ $-7 + 7 + x = -9 + 7.$ $x = -16.$

3. $20 - x = -14.$ $-20 + 20 - x = -14 - 20.$ $x = 34.$

4. $120 \cdot x = 314.$ $x = {}^{314}/_{120} = {}^{157}/_{60}.$

5. $75 \cdot x = 300.$ $x = {}^{300}/_{75} = 4.$

B.
1. $2(6) = 12$

2. $5(15) = 75$

3. $200(4) = 800.$

C.
1. $1 + [3 + (7-2)] = 1 + [3 + 5] = 1 + 8 = 9.$

2. $7 - [4(2)] = 7 - 8 = -1.$

3. $16(32-9) = 16(23) = 368.$

4. $5\{-3[4(2 \cdot 8)]\} = 5\{-3[4(16)]\} =$
   $5\{-3[64]\} = 5\{-192\} - 960.$

5. $1 + \{2[-3-(6+2)]\} = 1 + \{2[-3-6-2\} = 1 + \{2[-11]\}$
   $= 1 + -22 = 1 - 22 = -21.$

MORE COMPLEX EQUATIONS

1. $3xyz = 3(2.3) \cdot 4 \cdot 9 = 248.4.$

2. $2nz = 2(\sqrt{2}) \cdot -1 = -2.82.$

3. Numerical coefficient.

4. Variables.

5. (a) 2016
   (b) -462.2

6. 4th

7. (a) $x = 6y + 8.$

   (b) $c = \dfrac{38z - 14}{5}$ or, $7.6z - 2.8$

GRAPHING . . . LINEAR EQUATIONS

1. Function.

2. Cartesian coordinates.

3. Ordered pair.

4.
x	y
−2	−4
0	2
2	8
5	17

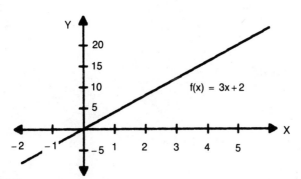

Fig. A-2

5.

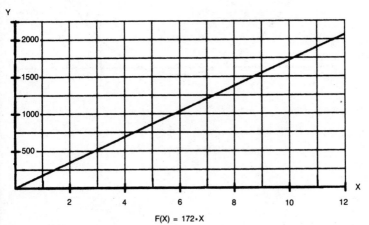

$F(X) = 172 * X$

Fig. A-3

123

HIGHER ORDER FUNCTIONS
THE QUADRATIC

1. $x^2 + 7x + 10$.

2. F O I L. First, outside, inside, last.

3. A quadratic.

4. Any equation possessing 5 as its highest exponent.

5. $ax^2 + bx + c = 0$.

6. $x = \dfrac{b \pm \sqrt{b^2 - 4ac}}{2a}$

7. 2

8. Discriminant

9. (a)

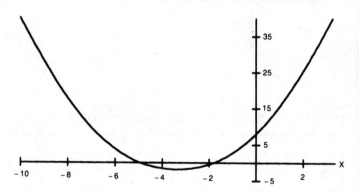

Fig. A-4

(b)

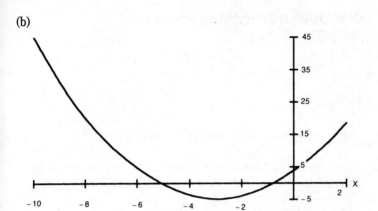

Fig. A-5

(c)

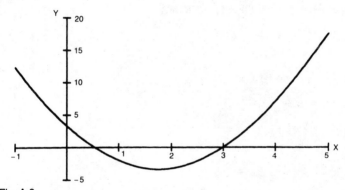

Fig. A-6

10. Imaginary.

11. $-16x^2 + 200x = 0.$

$$x = \frac{-b \pm \sqrt{b^2 - 4ac}}{2a} = \frac{-200 \pm \sqrt{200^2 - 4 \cdot -16 \cdot 1}}{2(-16)}$$

$$= \quad 0, \quad 12.5$$

a. $^{12.5}/_2 = 6^1/_4$ seconds to reach maximum altitude.
b. Maximum altitude = 625 ft.
c. Total flight time = 12.5 seconds.

POLYNOMIALS OF VARYING POWERS

1. $d^2 + 2de + e^2$

2. $c^3 + 3c^2b + 3cb^2 + b^3$

3. A sphere

4. $(n + m)^4 = n^4 + 4n^3m + 6n^2m^2 + 4nm^3 + m^4$

5. $(a + b)^2 \neq a^2 + b^2$ as $a^2 + b^2$ fails to incorporate the entire area. Substituting integers, we may indeed prove $a^2 + b^2$ to be inadequate: let $a = 3$, $b = 4$; $(a + b)^2 = (3 + 4)^2 = 9 + 16 = 25$. However, $3 + 4 = 7$, and $7^2 = 49$. 25 is only 51% of 49. However, the proper second degree expansion, $3^2 + 2(3 \cdot 4) + 4^2 = 9 + 24 + 16 = 49$.

MANIPULATION OF EQUATIONS

1. 400 mls.

2. $18.9 \approx 20$ mls.

3. 15 mls Con HNO_3.

4. $ab + c = -3.$ $\qquad a = {}^{-3-c/b}$

5. $C = 2\pi r.$ $\qquad r = {}^{C}/_{2\pi}$

Index

Other Bestsellers of Related Interest

ALGORITHMS ON GRAPHS—H. T. Lau

Here is a ready source of plug-in FORTRAN code for some of the most useful algorithms yet developed. You can use these efficient algorithms to solve almost any graphing problem dealing with the principles of: connectivity, shortest paths, minimum spanning tree, traversability, and node coloring. For each topic, you will find a description of the problem, an outline of the solution, an example, and a listing of the code used. You can use the programs just as they are—no problem-solving is required. 238 pages. Illustrated. Book No. 3429, $29.95 hardcover only

ELECTRONICS EQUATIONS HANDBOOK—Stephen J. Erst

Here is immediate access to equations for nearly every imaginable application! In this book, Stephen Erst provides an extensive compilation of formulas from his 40 years' experience in electronics. He covers 21 major categories and more than 600 subtopics in offering the over 800 equations. This broad-based volume includes equations in everything from basic voltage to microwave system designs. 280 pages, 219 illustrations. Book No. 3241, $16.95 paperback only

AC/DC ELECTRICITY & ELECTRONICS MADE EASY
—2nd Edition—Victor F. Veley

This completely revised and expanded edition of Victor Veley's classic electronics sourcebook has even more to offer than the bestselling first edition. Veley begins with thorough coverage of basic measurement units and leads you all the way through complex applications of waveform analysis. The latest material on decibels and nepers, filters, ac circuit analysis, motors, and nonsinusoidal waveforms is included. 370 pages, 205 illustrations. Book No. 3285, $17.95 paperback, $25.95 hardcover

BASIC ELECTRONICS THEORY—3rd Edition—Delton T. Horn

"All the information needed for a basic understanding of almost any electronic device or circuit . . ." was how *Radio-Electronics* magazine described the previous edition of this now-classic sourcebook. This completely updated and expanded edition provides a resource tool that belongs in a prominent place on every electronics bookshelf. Packed with illustrations, schematics, projects, and experiments, it's a book you won't want to miss! 544 pages, 650 illustrations. Book No. 3195, $21.95 paperback only

BASIC ELECTRONICS COURSE—2nd Edition—Norman H. Crowhurst

Absolutely no previous project building experience is necessary to assemble these devices! Projects include a pendulum clock, a siren, a music box, a photocell-activated night light, an audible continuity checker, a proximity detector, a one-IC AM radio and an electronic noise maker. This volume will introduce you to TTL and CMOS ICs, FETs, SCRs, Triacs, IR transmitters and receivers, and many other devices beyond the ordinary bipolar transistor. 400 pages, 347 illustrations. Book No. 2613, $17.95 paperback only

BEGINNER'S GUIDE TO READING SCHEMATICS
—Robert J. Traister

Electronics diagrams can be as easy to read as a road map with the help of this how-to handbook. You'll learn what each symbol stands for and what the cryptic words and numbers with each one mean. Block diagrams show where sections of complicated circuits are located and how they relate to each other, and flowcharts show you what should be happening where and when. 140 pages. 123 illustrations. Book No. 1536, $11.95 paperback only